America's Wild and Scenic
RIVERS

THE EAST FORK OF THE CARSON RIVER

Prepared by the Special Publications Division
National Geographic Society, Washington, D. C.

THE CLARKS FORK OF THE YELLOWSTONE RIVER

America's Wild and Scenic
RIVERS

America's Wild and Scenic Rivers

Contributing Authors: Louis de la Haba,
Toni Eugene, Lawrence F. Mosher,
Jennifer C. Urquhart

Contributing Photographers: Matt Bradley,
Richard A. Cooke III, Bill Curtsinger,
Steve Wall

Published by The National Geographic Society
Gilbert M. Grosvenor, *President*
Melvin M. Payne, *Chairman of the Board*
Owen R. Anderson, *Executive Vice President*
Robert L. Breeden, *Vice President, Publications and
Educational Media*

Prepared by The Special Publications Division
Donald J. Crump, *Editor*
Philip B. Silcott, *Associate Editor*
William L. Allen, William R. Gray, *Senior Editors*

Staff for this book
Mary Ann Harrell, *Managing Editor*
Thomas B. Powell III, *Picture Editor*
Jody Bolt, *Art Director*
Amy Goodwin, Alice K. Jablonsky,
Senior Researchers
Jane H. Buxton, Louis de la Haba, Toni Eugene,
Jennifer C. Urquhart, *Picture Legend Writers*
John D. Garst, Jr., Gary M. Johnson,
Judith Bell Siegel, Andrew J. Swithinbank,
Map Research and Production
Carol A. Rocheleau, *Illustrations Assistant*

Engraving, Printing, and Product Manufacture
Robert W. Messer, *Manager*
George V. White, *Production Manager*
Mary A. Bennett, *Production Project Manager*
Mark R. Dunlevy, Richard A. McClure,
David V. Showers, Gregory Storer, *Assistant
Production Managers;* Katherine H. Donohue,
Senior Production Assistant; Julia F. Warner,
Production Staff Assistant
Nancy F. Berry, Pamela A. Black, Mary
Elizabeth Davis, Claire M. Doig, Janet A.
Dustin, Rosamund Garner, Victoria D.
Garrett, Jane R. Halpin, Nancy J. Harvey,
Joan Hurst, Rebecca Bittle Johns, Artemis S.
Lampathakis, Katherine R. Leitch, Virginia
W. McCoy, Mary Evelyn McKinney, Cleo E.
Petroff, Tammy Presley, Sheryl A. Prohovich,
Kathleen T. Shea, *Staff Assistants*
Charles M. Israel, *Indexer*

*Divide Creek, spring-fed and pristine,
dashes to the Selway River in the immense
wilderness country of Idaho.*

HARDCOVER: THE NEW RIVER PLUNGES DOWN SANDSTONE FALLS IN
WEST VIRGINIA. JIM BRANDENBURG

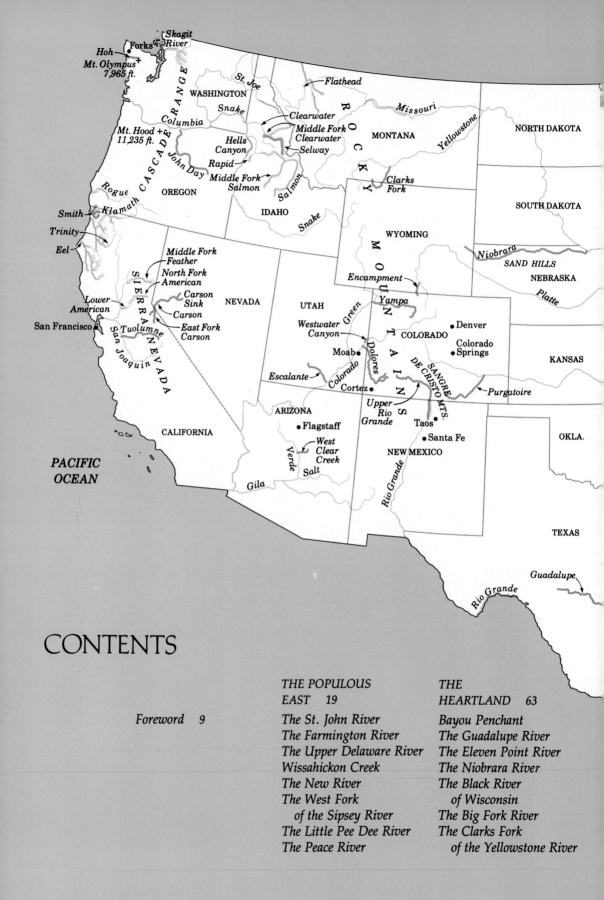

CONTENTS

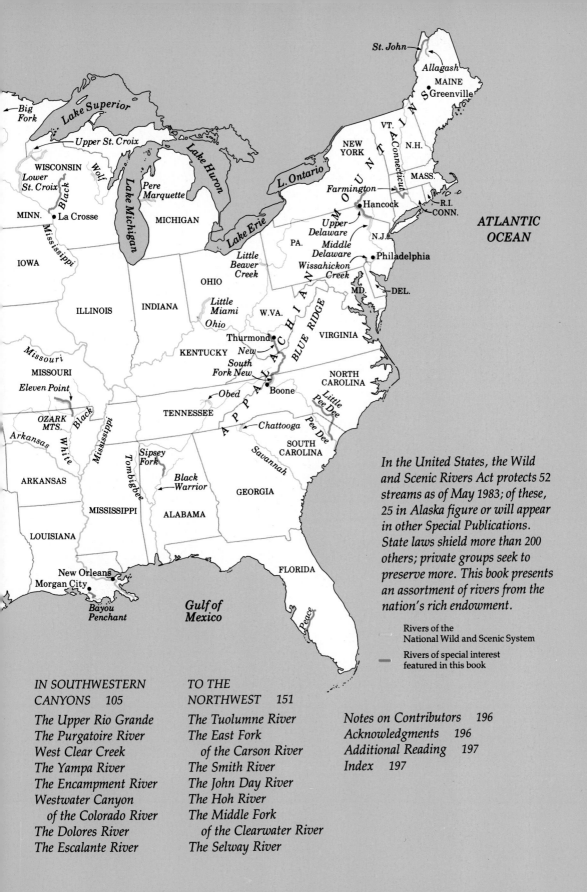

Big Fork

Lake Superior

Upper St. Croix

WISCONSIN

Lower St. Croix

Wolf

Black

Pere Marquette

Lake Michigan

Lake Huron

MICHIGAN

Lake Erie

L. Ontario

St. John

Allagash

MAINE

Greenville

VT.

N.H.

NEW YORK

Connecticut

MASS.

Farmington

Hancock

R.I.

CONN.

ATLANTIC OCEAN

MINN.

La Crosse

Mississippi

IOWA

ILLINOIS

INDIANA

OHIO

Little Beaver Creek

PA.

Upper Delaware

Middle Delaware

Wissahickon Creek

N.J.

Philadelphia

MD.

DEL.

Little Miami

Ohio

W.VA.

APPALACHIAN

BLUE RIDGE

Missouri

MISSOURI

Eleven Point

OZARK MTS.

Black

Arkansas

White

Mississippi

Thurmond

New

South Fork New

KENTUCKY

Obed

Boone

TENNESSEE

Chattooga

Sipsey Fork

Tombigbee

Black Warrior

VIRGINIA

NORTH CAROLINA

Little Pee Dee

Pee Dee

SOUTH CAROLINA

Savannah

ARKANSAS

MISSISSIPPI

ALABAMA

GEORGIA

LOUISIANA

New Orleans

Morgan City

Bayou Penchant

Gulf of Mexico

FLORIDA

Peace

In the United States, the Wild and Scenic Rivers Act protects 52 streams as of May 1983; of these, 25 in Alaska figure or will appear in other Special Publications. State laws shield more than 200 others; private groups seek to preserve more. This book presents an assortment of rivers from the nation's rich endowment.

Rivers of the National Wild and Scenic System

Rivers of special interest featured in this book

FOREWORD

How many splendid echoes this fine book awakens! The ancient Greek philosopher Heraclitus wrote, "It is not possible to step twice into the same river." My fascination with rivers does not go back quite that far, but it has lasted long enough for these pages to allow me a second step into many rivers that, man and boy, I have known intimately.

With rivers, "intimate" often means "soaking wet." But not always. I remember sunbaked schoolboy days in the late twenties and early thirties on the Potomac estuary. My brothers and I, lately from the dry Osage plains of southwest Missouri, felt drawn again and again to the lavish waters. On one outing, feeling bold, we nosed our canoe up the narrowing channel beyond the reach of tidewater and encountered for the first time the deep muscular dimension of a moving, living, freshwater force beneath us.

We were hooked for life. Ranging farther and farther, with a few friends, we began meeting the challenge of Middle Atlantic rivers, often marking off three- or four-day downriver runs, taking what the stream offered. Experience taught us; we learned the different paddle strokes before we knew what they were called. We saw no one else on the swift waters. Recreational use of rivers would build slowly toward the boom of the sixties. So when Congress passed the Wild and Scenic Rivers Act in 1968, and states enacted similar laws, it seemed simply an affirmation of what we had known and enjoyed all along.

The NATIONAL GEOGRAPHIC apparently had known it, too. Long before the Society added me to its staff 40 years ago, I read the magazine's exciting canoeing chronicles of Melville Chater and Amos Burg. In due course, I became acquainted with Amos Burg, who now, in his eighties, lives in retirement in Juneau. A recent exchange of letters recalls how I would look forward to the times when he came to Washington with a new manuscript or film. "And I would think," I wrote, "someday maybe I can emulate Amos Burg just a little."

My turn came, beginning in the late forties. On assignments for NATIONAL GEOGRAPHIC, various Society books, or the *Geographic School Bulletin,* my paddle planted swirl marks in many diverse rivers, including several featured in this book.

And so it is that the canoe paddle, speaking as it does of discovery, of history, of ultimate nature appreciation, becomes a baton to be passed along to the next relay of river-runners—so well represented by the keen adventurers and outstanding reporters and photographers in these pages. It is gratifying to know that yet another generation has accepted the challenge of America's wild and scenic rivers and has laid them before us in such style and spirit that readers will prove to old Heraclitus that indeed one may—at least vicariously—step again and again into the same river.

RALPH GRAY

Nearly engulfed by the roiling water of turbulent rapids, a raft passes 650 feet below the Rio Grande High Bridge near Taos, New Mexico.

*L*ike a crystalline curtain, the New River rushes through the Allegheny Plateau at Sandstone Falls, West Virginia. One of America's oldest rivers, the New has maintained a nearly unchanged course for about 200 million years.

*S*unday paddlers ruffle the smooth surface of the Eleven Point in southern Missouri. Since 1968 the Wild and Scenic Rivers Act has protected 44 miles of the stream's quiet water gliding through Ozark hills and hollows.

13

Formed of sand dunes that covered parts of the Southwest 200 million years ago, sheer walls of Wingate sandstone isolate the Dolores River near the Colorado-Utah border. Such rugged canyons surround the uplifted Uncompahgre Plateau.

Catching the morning sun, Idaho's Selway River snakes through thickly forested canyons. Beargrass opens the regal orbs of its white flowers to greet the arrival of spring. These plants bloom erratically every five to seven years.

Splashing over a rocky ledge, the South Fork of the New River begins its course northwest through the ancient Appalachian Mountains near Boone, North Carolina. For 250 miles, the New threads through wilderness forest, tranquil farmlands, and a spectacular gorge. Federal and state laws help preserve portions of the historic stream in North Carolina and West Virginia.

By Louis de la Haba
Photographed by Bill Curtsinger

The
Populous East

When spring comes to Maine's remote north woods, it's as if someone had opened a storm drain for the frozen St. John River. Huge blocks of ice break off in the accelerating flow and crash against the trunks of spruces, poplars, and birches along the banks, leaving raw scars high on the bark. It seems impossible now, only a few weeks after the first thaw, that the river could ever have been so high.

But "now" is the beginning of June, and we have to get out of our canoes and drag them over the riverbed to deeper water. "Frogging," Alexandra Conover calls this uncongenial task. "Frogging," as in "we'll have to frog that bony section over there." When things get really trying, she calls it "bull frogging." Bony? That means the water is shallow and strewn with rocks.

Alexandra is one of our guides on the St. John; the other is her husband, Garrett, a tall, bushy-bearded man in his late 20s. My colleague and friend, photographer Bill Curtsinger, is the fourth member of our group.

What has the densely settled East to offer as riverside wilderness? Bill and I will visit eight of its streams during the next few months, and find the St. John the most nearly pristine. Yet even on the St. John, out of the way and hard to reach though it is, the works of man are all too often evident.

One rainy morning, we had met Alexandra and Garrett at Greenville, on Moosehead Lake, for a floatplane trip over forest—largely owned by paper companies—where the only roads are private. When the rain let up to a thin drizzle, we took off for Fifth St. John Pond.

Our river is born of a series of ponds, beginning with First and ending with Fifth. It wanders north and east through Maine and Canada to enter the Bay of Fundy at St. John, New Brunswick. At Fifth St. John the little plane leaves us and our two cedar-ash-and-canvas canoes of classic E. M. White design. This craft, with a round keelless bottom, rides high in the water, perfect for the shallows and rapids we'll encounter over 145 miles. We load the canoes with wicker pack baskets full of supplies for nine days, the wanigan—a wooden box containing all the cooking equipment—and our personal gear, stowed in waterproof bags.

We paddle to the embankment of an abandoned dam and set up our camp under a clearing sky and a rising breeze that rids the air of blackflies and mosquitoes. I watch three loons dawdling in the pond. From its perch in a spruce tree, a white-throated sparrow sweetly whistles for "Poor Sam Peabody, Peabody, Peabody." And next morning we begin our journey in earnest.

Below the old dam, the St. John—here called Baker Branch—is shallow and swift. Before long we have to get out to frog. Many of the submerged rocks are marked with blue, red, green, yellow, or aluminum where previous travelers have scraped their canoes. Garrett says these rocks have "a rainbow history."

On both sides the forest is thick with balsam firs and spruce interspersed with birches and alders. Birds are plentiful. We see or hear tree swallows, water thrushes, winter wrens, parula warblers, rose-breasted grosbeaks, veeries, grackles, mergansers, and hawks: broad-winged, red-tailed, and Cooper's. Flowers—white bunchberries and starflowers, mostly—bloom on the banks and in the woods. We feel we are deep in the wilderness, but the feeling is deceptive. In places it takes just a few minutes' bushwhacking up the bank to find large areas of clear-cutting, where every tree, large or small, has been machine-clipped down to the ground.

This troubles the Conovers. As Alexandra tells me, "It's really difficult when you bring people out for a wilderness experience and you know full well that just past the immediate scene there are places where skidders are taking out timber, or mechanical harvesters are clear-cutting the forest." Skidders are big diesel-powered, log-hauling machines. Their noise can be heard for miles, Alexandra says.

We're no longer paddling. Garrett and Alexandra are standing up in the sterns of the canoes, skillfully guiding them with long steel-shod spruce poles. If you're experienced enough with a pole, you can stop a canoe anywhere, even in the middle of a rapid. You can also pole upstream, and when canoes were a principal means of transport, people often did.

The St. John alternates between stretches of mild rapids and longish pools of calm water. In the Maine woods, according to Garrett and Alexandra, a small rapid is a "rip." Calm water is "dead," and backwaters are called "logans," or "bogans," from an old lumbermen's term. As elsewhere, eddies are countercurrents, where the water curls around behind a rock and flows upstream. These are safe places to nose into and take time out to plan your course.

One evening we camp in a grassy area bordered by tall trees. Garrett says it's a "stately avenue of poplars." Moose have been here, cropping the tender buds of alder bushes. We hear a ruffed grouse drumming—a particularly penetrating beat you can feel in your throat as if your heart were racing off on a runaway pulse. The night begins to get cool and breezy.

"Louis, get up!" Bill calls next morning. "The frost is on the pun'kin—it's all over your tent." My tent has turned white, and everything outside is damp with melting rime. The sun is shining through the treetops; lacy veils of mist rise from the river. Bill has been up since dawn, taking pictures. Garrett comes over to watch and comments on the "tendrils of mist." "That's it!" Bill says delightedly. "Tendrils of mist!" The phrase soon becomes a byword for his early morning sessions with the cameras.

As we approach Baker Lake, we spot two loons swimming a short distance ahead. They are big, handsome birds with their black heads, white collars, and black-and-white reticulated backs. Sometimes they submerge just beneath the surface, with their heads showing like periscopes on submarines. When we enter the lake, a sharp breeze has come up. Fortunately for us, it's not a head wind, but we have a difficult two-mile paddle along the length of the lake.

Downstream, the river will be joined by major tributaries, the Southwest Branch and then the Northwest Branch. It will become much wider and, we hope, deeper. Here it's still shallow, and we're gingerly picking our way through the rips. At the next campsite, we find our first fellow travelers, their canoes (Continued on page 26)

21

*N*orth-woods guide Alexandra Conover poles the author through a rapid on Maine's remote St. John River. In nine days she and her husband, Garrett (below), took him and photographer Bill Curtsinger through 145 miles of river travel. Below, Garrett's boot holds a wood frog that simply hopped aboard.

FOLLOWING PAGES: *Dawn's first light gilds a softly misted St. John. Spruces, firs, white pines, and hardwoods that line the banks form a 2.5-million-acre forest that extends to the Canadian border.*

pulled up on the high bank. We feel infringed upon, but, of course, we're the infringers. It's cold again. Dark clouds loom from the south.

"Those clouds," Garrett proclaims, "are descending with great descenditude." He likes to talk like that.

Our own descenditude is taking us deeper into country described in the *Nationwide Rivers Inventory* as the "largest and least accessible and most primitive geographical units east of the Mississippi River." As the days pass, we see more and more wildlife—more birds, wood turtles basking on muddy banks, deer here and there. Unexpectedly one morning we come upon a moose, a young male, standing in the middle of the river. He sees us; he twitches his big ears, but holds his ground. We approach slowly, and the moose skittishly turns away. Finally he breaks, trotting over the uneven riverbed, and scrambles up the bank. Bill, cameras always at hand, has been clicking away as we draw near. I think what an easy shot it would be for a hunter.

Our frogging, poling, and paddling continue as the river begins to take on a different aspect, widening even more, with higher banks. Low hills covered with spruce and fir, aspen, poplars, and birches mark our horizon. For a few days our precarious solitude is broken by crop dusters whose pilots regale us with morning air shows. They are spraying the spruce budworms that are ravaging so much of the Maine woods. At Red Pine, where we stop for lunch, we find their base—a macadam strip, a few sheds, three spotter planes, six crop dusters, and a tanker truck filled with Sevin-4-Oil, the stuff that kills the pests. The planes are grounded today; it's too windy for spraying.

Every once in a while, when we stop for lunch or when we take out for the day, Garrett will unlimber his fly rod and start fishing. There're no fish in the St. John, he proclaims. This is simply an incantation he hopes will fool the fish. Much of the time it doesn't, but sometimes we get a bit of trout with our supper.

So far, the river has been kindly, and we're making good progress. On the seventh day, we approach the first major rapid—Big Black—just upstream from where the Big Black River joins the St. John from the west. But as we enter the mile-and-a-quarter rapid, we find the water is too low for a really good run.

The St. John is considered impassable when its flow is less than 3,000 cfs, cubic feet per second or cusecs, at the Dickey Gauging Station. On the day we went through Big Black Rapids, the flow was just under that—2,964 cfs—and for the remainder of our trip, around a meager 2,000. Normal spring flow is 12,000 to 14,000 cusecs; it has run as high as 70,000. In contrast, the record summertime low is 129. To paddle the St. John, you have to be there at the right time.

We get proof of that below the Big Black confluence. Now the current is stronger, and the river widens to perhaps a thousand feet. We find it so shallow that Garrett and Alexandra wince when the shellacked hulls of their beautiful canoes scrape against rocks and gravel. On our last night in the wilderness, the flies, mosquitoes, and gnats are fierce; we make short work of supper. Tomorrow will be a big day: We'll take on Big Rapids—the most turbulent of all on the St. John— and we'll reach civilization as well. I'm not looking forward to that.

The day dawns clear and warm. We shift from paddling to poling,

poling to paddling, at Long Rapids, Castonia, Schoolhouse, and Fox Brook Rapids. On the accepted scale of difficulty these are usually Class I or Class II—easy going—with adequate water. At extreme high water they do not exist; at such low water as we find them, they require poling—and patience. We back and sideslip and wriggle slowly along a tortuous channel in a foot of water or less. We have lunch at Fox Brook, and Garrett catches a fine brook trout.

Finally we come to Big Rapids, after a sweeping bend that takes us about the compass from southeast to northwest to northeast. According to our map, we'll drop somewhere between 40 and 60 feet in only two and a quarter miles. These rapids generally rank as Class III, which implies a risk of swamping for loaded open canoes like ours. Even at low water the river is roaring. It is cluttered with ledges and heavy waves, and huge boulders dwarf Alexandra's standing figure as she steers her canoe ahead of ours through quick and at times radical maneuvers. We get a thrill—and a splashing—going through.

At one point, the tip of Garrett's pole jams between two rocks. He has taken the calculated risk of cross-body poling. Now the pole is wedged across his chest; he risks breaking it or being swept off the canoe, possibly tipping it over. He jumps off. Sitting up forward, intent on the water, I don't even know he's gone. Alexandra has checked her canoe at a less turbulent spot; she glances around, sees him, and shouts to me. I look behind me, find myself without a sternman, and backpaddle as hard as I can—an instinctive, useless gesture. Quickly, Alexandra steers her canoe toward mine, and Bill grabs it; her pole "anchors" both boats while Garrett dislodges his. He splashes through hip-deep water, steps up on a rock, and comes aboard, dripping cold water and looking a little sheepish. "I had to jump," he says apologetically. We all laugh with relief, and the man of eloquent expression says nothing more about it.

At Dickey we put in to shore and are met by Wilmer Hafford, a friend of the Conovers who has been watching for us. He drives us to a store where Bill and I get cold drinks and make some phone calls. A hefty fellow in his 30s, Wilmer is a true Maine Yankee, a man of few words, each carefully considered. Bill asks him what people here think about the Dickey-Lincoln Hydroelectric Project, a proposal to dam the St. John to generate power for peak demand periods.

Wilmer ponders for a while and says: "We-el, some are for it, and some are agin' it." When he gets to know us a little better he reveals his own opinion: that a smaller dam on a tributary stream would be enough to meet local needs.

On our last reach of the day we pass the mouth of another famous white-water river—the Allagash, part of the nation's Wild and Scenic System—and the sites for the Dickey-Lincoln dams. Then a phone call from the store at St. Francis brings a single-engine Beaver that lands on the St. John and whisks us over the wilderness to Greenville.

Later I hear that "agin' it" has prevailed. Dickey-Lincoln's two dams would have flooded 86,000 acres along 55 miles of river, a loss environmentalists and others found unacceptable. By 1982 estimates,

Fall's leafy confetti piles up in an eddy behind rocks on the Farmington River in western Connecticut. Cradled by wooded hills, the Farmington murmurs over the green and peaceful countryside. Mills and factories once heavily polluted a river that today runs clean and almost clear. Its frothy rapids, especially at Satan's Kingdom and Tariffville Gorge, provide a challenging training ground for world-class kayakers and canoeists. Trout and the annual springtime run of shad lure anglers from the heavily populated area around nearby Hartford. In an ambitious program, state biologists attempt, with some success, to bring back the long-absent Atlantic salmon, prized by gourmets and fishermen alike.

the project would have cost about a billion dollars, and yet—operating an average of three hours a day—would have produced barely one percent of New England's power.

Even so, I find myself wondering about the future of the St. John. Dams can have serious unforeseen—and unforeseeable—effects on the life of any river. The Farmington is a good example.

Rising in the Berkshire Hills of Massachusetts, the 87-mile-long Farmington flows generally south and east into Connecticut, where it joins the Connecticut River. Today it graces the green and gentle New England countryside with its clear cascading water, its wooded banks, and its two swiftwater gorges, Tariffville Gorge and Satan's Kingdom.

There's still some way to go before the Farmington's water can be called pure. But around 1870 conditions were much worse. Paper mills, tanneries, cotton mills, sawmills, and foundries all dumped their effluvia into the river, so polluting it that few fish survived. The "Great Decline" that struck western Connecticut late in the century forced many of the mills and factories to close, but at least it improved the quality of the water.

I went canoeing on the Farmington with Culver Modisette, a former advertising executive and avid outdoorsman, president of the Farmington River Watershed Association. Since its founding in 1953 this group has been concerned with protecting and improving the river. We put in at Riverton, just across from the Old Riverton Inn, an establishment that has been catering to travelers since 1796.

In midsummer, the water was low, but we had to frog only twice. It was a pleasant day, cool and overcast, and we had the river almost to ourselves, except for a few fishermen standing in midstream with their waders and fly rods. There were many small rapids, all easy. Culver told me how local municipalities and industry are working to eliminate pollution entirely, and how a recent referendum had defeated a proposal to divert the upper river to take more water to the nearby Hartford metropolitan area.

"The most exciting thing I can tell you about the Farmington is that the Atlantic salmon is coming back," Culver said. The powerful, silvery salmon, sometimes called the king of fishes, vanished from the river two centuries ago, when milldams blocked its spawning runs upstream. Then, in 1978, came a sign of change. Salmon started coming back. The first salmon was spotted through the observation window of the fishway at Rainbow Dam on May 24. Stephen R. Gephard remembers it well; he's a Connecticut state biologist on duty at the fishway. Steve and his associates promptly captured the salmon and removed it to a holding station. There, the fish and others that followed were kept until spawning time in November. After the eggs hatched, the young fry were kept for two years.

Paddling solo, Garrett Conover maneuvers his canoe through Skinners Falls, a demanding rapid on the Upper Delaware National Scenic and Recreational River, a 73-mile stretch of wooded hills on the New York-Pennsylvania border.

As they approached the age of "smolting," when changes in physiology prepare them for life in salt water, they were taken to Rainbow. Before being released to the sea, they spent several weeks in imprinting ponds filled with water from the Farmington.

Steve believes that the first fish to return had figured in a similar procedure in 1976. Then rivers in Canada and Maine had supplied the fertilized eggs. "Imprinting is the key to the program," Steve explained. "Salmon don't hatch 'knowing' the way home by instinct. It's the smell of the water—they learn it as young fish and home to it as adults. By imprinting them with Farmington water we actually fooled Penobscot River fish into thinking they were Farmington fish."

Progress has been somewhat slow. Fifty-six salmon were captured at Rainbow in 1978, 32 in 1979, only 26 in 1980, 62 in 1981. For 1985, however, Steve expects 700 to 800 returns, and more after that.

Rivers are like people; each has a unique character and personality. Perhaps this is why they have such a special appeal for writers. Of the Farmington, Henry James wrote that it was an "ample, admirable, in every way distinguished" stream. Zane Grey, although famous for his tales of the West, was an admirer of another eastern river, the upper Delaware of New York and Pennsylvania. His first published work was an article entitled "A Day on the Delaware." It was about fishing.

I visited the Zane Grey House, on the bank of the Delaware at Lackawaxen, Pennsylvania, and there found a letter Grey had written to his friend Alvah D. James in 1933: "Just to get your letter made me see the old familiar places as vividly as if I had been there. I could see the October colors of the hills and the old Delaware winding down from the mountains, and the purple asters blumbing [Grey's spelling was a little weak] along the trails, the smokey Indian summer colors and the smell of the pine."

Helen James Davis, daughter of Alvah James, has opened the Grey house to the public—a house full of memorabilia, letters, books, and even Grey's daunting instruments. He was a dentist before he became known as a writer.

"He wrote at least 85 books, all of them in pencil and all of them in longhand, 13 of them right here in this room. If he made $37,000,000, he spent $36,000,000 fishing," Mrs. Davis told me. Fishing is a major sport on the upper Delaware—for trout, for shad during the annual spring run, and for bass, pickerel, and walleye. Eels are caught here in long V-shaped stone weirs.

On the upper Delaware, a 73-mile stretch between the town of Hancock, New York, and Port Jervis ranks as a national scenic and recreational river. Thus the National Park Service has a key role in setting policy for the stream, with state and local authorities cooperating. This area is unique in that the federal government plans to purchase only some 156 acres of the 86,000 designated for the park. The rest is, for the most part, privately owned. Along the forested banks stand towns and villages with old houses of great charm, some in Greek Revival, Italianate, and Queen Anne styles.

The other major sport on the upper Delaware is canoeing.

Because it is close to metropolitan areas—New York City lies within 125 miles—this is a heavily used river. "There are 26 canoe liveries in the park now, two of them the largest in the country and, among them, they are capable of putting more than 4,000 canoes in the water at one time," chief ranger Ron Wilson of the National Park Service told me. "You can see how that might create some problems for us."

Ron and I spent one Saturday afternoon at Skinners Falls, the most popular rapids on the upper Delaware. We sat on the rocks among a crowd of people who came to watch the fun. At a livery upstream from us, canoeists were putting in by the dozen. Down they came in bunches, paddling wildly, and hitting the rapids with whoops and hollers worthy of a Zane Grey story.

Skinners Falls is not a particularly difficult run, if you know what you're doing. The experienced canoeists made it through easily. But many were clearly beginners, out for an afternoon away from the city. Nearly a dozen canoes rammed into the rocks and tipped over, throwing occupants and contents into the rushing stream. Red-capped volunteers from the National Canoe Safety Patrol went to the rescue in their own canoes, pulling people aboard and taking them ashore, and getting the capsized craft off the rocks.

A pileup occurred when a canoe became pinned broadside against a rock and another crashed into it. I watched tensely while park rangers and volunteers got everyone out safely. When a canoe gets trapped against an obstacle, it creates a very dangerous situation. For example, a ten-mile-an-hour current can put a four-ton pressure on a canoe; if the paddlers get caught between the rock and the canoe they can be gravely injured, or killed. There were ten boating-related deaths in the park in 1980, but thanks to alert rescuers and to a vigorous water-safety campaign, the number was reduced to one in 1981 and one in 1982—of more than eighty thousand at risk.

Once regarded as wild, unappealing, and inadequate for agriculture, the upper valley of the Delaware was not extensively settled until late in the 19th century. Before the Revolution, the area was the subject of conflicting land claims from New York, New Jersey, and Pennsylvania. Earlier still, the wide-ranging Iroquois Confederacy had enjoyed power here. The inhabitants were the Munsey (or Minsi) Indians, a subgroup of the Indians called Delaware by the English and Lenape, Real Persons, by themselves.

The Lenape were peaceful villagers who relied on corn crops as well as hunting, fishing, and gathering wild foodstuffs. According to local tradition, one of their favorite hunting grounds was along a wooded creek that now flows near the heart of Philadelphia. Wissahickon Creek has cut ravines that a Baedeker guidebook once admiringly compared to an "Alpine gorge in miniature." Supposedly it gets its name from a blend of two Lenape words meaning "yellow-colored stream" and "catfish stream."

The Wissahickon's outcrops of ancient rocks—gneisses, and mica- and garnet-bearing schists—inspired the famed 19th-century actress Fanny Kemble to flights of poetry and the poet Edgar Allan Poe to romantic prose. Wrote Kemble in a lyric of farewell: "Never from stony rifts of granite grey/ Sparkling like diamond rocks in the Sun's

"*A little gem of a creek,*" *the author calls the Wissahickon, a bubbling stream that runs near the heart of Philadelphia. The creek cascades over an old mill dam, a memento of its industrial past, but with the mills gone, the lower Wissahickon has gradually returned to its natural state. Part of the city's Fairmount Park, the Wissahickon Valley's wooded glades and paths offer a respite from the clamor of the nearby city. A horse feeds near a restored 1890 Brewster Bronson carriage at Monastery Stable. This riding club occupies the grounds of a now vanished religious community founded by 18th-century German immigrants who used the creek's waters for their baptismal rites.*

ray/ Shall I look down on thee, thou pleasant stream/ Beneath whose crystal folds the gold sands gleam."

And one day, while floating lazily in a skiff, Poe savored "visions of the Wissahiccon of ancient days . . . when the red man trod alone, with the elk, upon the ridges that now towered above." He wrote of an elk "standing upon the extreme verge of the precipice, with neck outstretched, with ears erect, and with the whole attitude indicative of profound and melancholy inquisitiveness. . . ." Poe actually saw an elk—an old, tame animal belonging to a neighborhood family.

There are no elk on the Wissahickon today, but the beauty of the place exceeds that of Poe's time, when paper mills and gristmills used the creek's water. The creek retains its wild aspect in the midst of urban bustle partly because it lies within the city's Fairmount Park and partly because of the continuing vigilance of the Friends of the Wissahickon, an organization founded in 1925.

I toured the valley with its president, F. Markoe Rivinus, a native Philadelphian who lives on the edge of the park. While we walked some of the trails, he pointed out particularly attractive vistas and items of interest. By car we visited such places as the so-called Monastery, a house built about 1745 by one Joseph Gorgas, a German immigrant and Seventh Day Baptist leader, and the nearby Baptisterion, a pool where converts were thrice immersed in the cool waters of the creek. At the Andorra Natural Area, a note pinned to the bulletin board listed the "week's observations": "Deer have their fawns now, hidden in the thickets . . . a buck with velveted antlers was in the upper fields area twice this week . . . there is a phoebe nesting in the old barn. Does anyone know if the birds are still there?"

Next morning, alone, I climbed a steepish trail to a stone statue of a brooding Lenape, tomahawk in his left hand, right hand shading his eyes, staring westward. Several thousand representatives of his people, I recalled, reside in Oklahoma, Wisconsin, and Ontario today. I continued my walk through the muted woods, under a canopy of white and red oaks, beeches, sycamores, and tulip trees, and crossed the creek by a covered bridge, last of its kind in the valley. I heard the screech of bluejays and saw the iridescent flash of a kingfisher in flight. A few early morning joggers and walkers and a young woman on a horse were the only people about.

One last time I drove a zigzag course over the bridges high above the creek. Again I marveled that such a wilderness could exist so close to the heart of Megalopolis. I was grateful that it does.

If the Wissahickon's is a "miniature" gorge, that of the New River is a mighty one by any standard applicable to eastern rivers. The New begins a northward course near the summits of the Blue Ridge in North Carolina, meanders among rugged hills and fertile farmlands, and goes on to Virginia and West Virginia. There it cuts through the western Appalachians and, 250 miles from its beginning, joins the tumultuous Gauley River to form the Kanawha, a tributary of the Ohio.

To conform to the pattern for eastern rivers, the waters of the New should end up in the Atlantic. Instead, they enter the drainage system of the Mississippi. This is due to the New's great antiquity: It can be traced to the Jurassic period, around 180 million years ago. Then it was, apparently, the main headwaters branch of a now-extinct river that geologists call the Teays, which flowed westward to an inland sea. Over millions of years, the highlands were eroded into a plain, which in turn was uplifted and folded. Since the New wore down its bed more rapidly than the mountains rose, it continued to cut through the slowly rising ground and held its westward course unchanged.

Today its strength—and age—are most obvious between Hinton and Gauley Bridge, West Virginia, where the New passes through a heavily wooded gorge. This varies in depth from 600 feet near Hinton to 1,400 feet near Grandview State Park. At Fayette Station a spectacular single-arch steel bridge crosses the river. The Washington Monument, 555 feet tall, could stand below this span with 320 feet to spare; and the view from this bridge is, to say the least, impressive.

Bill Curtsinger and I traced most of the New from its headwaters to Gauley Bridge and found it a river of many faces and moods. We cannot call it a wilderness river. Many people live along its banks, farm its floodplains, use its waters for fishing and other sports, and—in some reaches—let it carry off their trash. It is not a free-flowing river. Three dams interrupt its passage, one in Virginia and two in West Virginia. Yet in many respects it is indeed wild.

Our first glimpse of it came after a steep descent from the Blue Ridge Parkway, where we had admired the constantly changing vistas of hazy, ragged ridges superimposed one upon another in pastel tints of purples, blues, and grays. We drove to Boone—named after the redoubtable Dan'l, who explored, hunted, and lived among these hills—and there picked up the South Fork.

Since 1976, North Carolina has administered the affairs of the South Fork as a component of the National Wild and Scenic Rivers System. Earlier, the state helped defeat a power company's plan to build a dam that would have flooded more than 40 miles of the New River itself, 23 miles of the North Fork, and 24 miles of the South.

Just east of Boone, we found our river to be narrow and shallow. There were many riffles and small rapids where the water whispered in frothy plumes past thickly wooded banks. Two-lane country roads followed the stream in places; crossed and recrossed it in others.

We traveled these roads for several days, almost always within view of the growing, widening stream. We stopped often to explore and to enjoy the sight of the mountains, of peaceful riverside farms where cattle grazed, of children floating downstream on inner tubes. We saw fields where young tobacco plants were growing gold-green in the high summer sun and others where neatly spaced hayricks cast patterns of light and shadow on the river's stubbled bank.

For 30 straight-line miles—the figure is deceptive; there are few straight lines in these parts—the South Fork meanders within its valley until it meets the North Fork near the (Continued on page 48)

FOLLOWING PAGES: *Nearly buried by a wall of water, a raftful of paddlers plows through a rapid on the New River near Thurmond, West Virginia, one of the most popular stretches of white water in the eastern United States.*

Summertime heaven: a deep pool, a rock to jump from, and friends to share the fun. With white water that challenges the skill of experts, the New also holds quiet pleasures for the lone traveler or the family that goes camping.

FOLLOWING PAGES: *Ferns and mossy boulders surround a fallen sweet gum tree in a mist-filled glen at Grandview State Park, on the New River Gorge.*

Headed for the New River's roughest white water, two rafts pass under the bridge at Thurmond. Once a thriving railroad town and a major center for the New River coalfields, Thurmond now attracts rafters, kayakers, and canoeists.

FOLLOWING PAGES: *Coal miner Sidney Ward and "Blackie" contemplate the river from the C&O tracks. "The gorge has to be seen to be appreciated," says Mr. Ward. "The sky, hills, and river all seem to blend into one beautiful picture."*

Virginia border. At the confluence I saw canoeists on the water, and couldn't help imagining a lake agitated by fast and noisy outboards.

Coming into Virginia, where it begins its crossing of the higher Appalachian ranges, the New meets its first major man-made obstruction, Claytor Dam, near the small city of Radford. Beyond, at Hinton, another dam controls the now-considerable flow. Bluestone Dam, a flood-control structure operated by the U. S. Army Corps of Engineers, impounds the New into ten-mile-long Bluestone Lake. To keep the lake level constant, attendants hold back water or release it into the lower river, causing wide fluctuations in the flow below the dam and disturbing fishermen, rafters, and canoeists.

The southern boundary of the New River Gorge National River is just a couple of miles below the dam, and there Bill and I began a four-day exploration of the gorge. Our guides and rubber rafts were provided by an outfitter based at Thurmond.

On our first day we encountered two formidable obstacles, Brooks Falls and Sandstone Falls. We could have made it down Brooks, but our guides decided to keep us dry and lined the raft over the steep pitch with ropes. At Sandstone, a roaring, crescent-shaped waterfall that attracts many campers, fishermen, and picnickers, there is a shallow passage on the west side, and we frogged our raft over that. For the next three days we became intimate with the river. So intimate, in fact, that at one point we spent almost an hour in it.

This happened during one of those ferocious storms that assault the Appalachians on summer afternoons and make the narrow valleys reverberate with thunder. Torrential rain fell on us, and the wind whipped the river into whitecaps. We sought shelter on shore, but the riverbank was so steep and so muddy that we could hardly keep our footing. The rain was so cold that we finally jumped into the river's slightly warmer water as the better of two unattractive alternatives. We were a sorry, sodden bunch when we reached Thurmond.

At one time or another between the 1880s and the 1950s there were 30-odd towns along the New River Gorge, for 27 mining operations working the area's famed high-grade, smokeless coal. Only three exist today, and one of these, Thurmond, was something more than a coal town.

Thurmond thrived as a railroad center whose main street was, and still is, the main line of the Chesapeake & Ohio Railway. Trains of a hundred cars or more constantly roar through the gorge here, hauling out coal as well as transporting chemicals, heavy equipment, and routine freight. Six times a week there are Amtrak passenger trains as well, and all of them make the hills echo with the clatter of wheels and the blast of air horns.

A community of pious teetotalers, Thurmond tried to keep the

Blunt-bowed johnboat nudges the bank of the West Fork, Sipsey River, below 80-foot sandstone cliffs. Deep within the Bankhead National Forest in Alabama, the Sipsey Wilderness encompasses 12,726 acres of undisturbed woodland.

riffraff outside the city limits. Still, it became notorious as a sort of Dodge City of the coalfields—a place of raucous saloons and brothels, and of explosive violence. Once it had as many as 500 residents; today it has only 67. But the growing interest in rafting and the gorge's new status as a national river have brought many visitors in the past few years, and the number will doubtless increase. By National Park Service estimate, some 52,000 people made the white-water run between Thurmond and Fayette Station in 1981, using the services of commercial outfitters. Another 3,000 made the run on their own.

From Thurmond downriver to Fayette Station, the New has cut the most spectacular part of its gorge, a chasm walled by massive sandstone cliffs that offers some of the best white water in the east. It channels a series of ten major and many minor rapids, and has become a magnet for rafters and kayakers—daring kayakers.

We ran these rapids on our last day on the New, racing down precipitous pitches and ramming into huge waves that momentarily submerged us and left our rafts clumsy and full of water. We bailed, paddled vigorously to keep control of the lurching craft, sped past dangerous undercut ledges, and gratefully stopped for lunch, all cold and wet. In the afternoon, we went through more rapids with names like Double Z, Old 99 Hook, and Greyhound Bus Stopper, and took out at Fayette Station, almost directly under that high steel bridge.

The rapids are the reason why most visitors come to the New. But in my opinion, the river's most precious treasure lies upstream, where a creek flows in through a concrete culvert that runs under the railroad tracks. This dark, slippery, uninviting tunnel gives admission into a miniature paradise beyond.

Once past the tunnel we followed the little stream for a few yards into a rocky bower filled with maples, hickories, birches, and tulip poplars. A wide waterfall shaped a silver curtain at the back of this natural amphitheater; mosses and ferns carpeted the ground. Liz Watson, one of our guides, pointed out a boulder near the bottom of the waterfall. On its surface I could see embedded the shells of fossil brachiopods, clamlike creatures abundant here 300 million years ago. "Every time I come here," Liz said, "whole layers have weathered off the rock, and new fossils are exposed."

We climbed a steep trail on our left, past a snail that was feasting on a mushroom and a late-blooming rhododendron that had shed its waxy-white petals on the mossy ground, and came to another, smaller grotto. Here a ribbon waterfall cascaded into a deep pool with such force that it shattered into a fine mist. Glittering droplets shone on the leaves of trees, the lacy fronds of ferns, and the moss- and lichen-covered rocks. A centipede was creeping along, metallic black-and-gold, and two bright-orange efts of spotted newt clung to rocks. Sunlight barely penetrated the trees' canopy overhead. Bill spoke quietly: "I could stay here for days."

As we progressed to other rivers, we found other hidden places where, adventuring off the main flow or off a well-worn path, we came upon unexpected beauty. Such a river is the Sipsey Fork, a branch of the Black Warrior River in northwestern Alabama. Formally called the West Fork, Sipsey River, it flows through the Sipsey

Wilderness, a part of the William B. Bankhead National Forest. The forest honors a distinguished legislator, who was the father of the noted actress Tallulah Bankhead. To my knowledge, Miss Bankhead never wrote poems about the Sipsey Fork, but we can wish she had.

Like Fanny Kemble's Wissahickon, the Sipsey is a delightful stream that has carved another miniature gorge. Deep in the wildest part of the national forest, its clear waters run through silent woods that include thirteen species of oak, four each of hickory and pine, three of elm, two of gum and maple, and other trees, including catalpa, holly, locust, poplar, sourwood, walnut, and willow.

With Steve McCorquodale, the ranger in charge of the forest's Black Warrior District, I hiked through portions of the wilderness while he explained how climate and topography had combined to make this a meeting place for northern and southern species, so that northern trees such as sugar maple grow near such preeminently southern ones as catalpa.

The Sipseys, river and wilderness, have their hidden riches, and Steve showed us to two of them. One was the forest's prize tree, the biggest poplar in Alabama, a majestic specimen standing by itself near a cliff and waterfall. Steve took a D-tape out of his pack, and I held one end against the trunk while he walked around it. A D-tape is a forester's tool that converts circumference directly into diameter. It read 80.3 inches—a shade over 6 feet, 6 inches. I looked toward the top of the tree, outlined against the clouds of a gathering storm, and Steve told me the poplar was 150 feet tall.

The second was a dazzling little cove we reached while canoeing on the Sipsey. We had been paddling for about five miles under towering sandstone cliffs when we came to the mouth of a narrow creek on our left. We entered the creek, rounded a couple of bends, and came into a shady pool rimmed by high rocks and trees. On the far wall, the crystal ribbon of a waterfall tumbled from an overhang and splashed against the rocks at the bottom. We watched in silence and, as on the New, I felt as though the river had granted us a gift.

All through this remote hill country there are old cemeteries, abandoned settlements, and, as I was told by Mickey Linley of the Forest Service, the remains of abandoned stills. "A lot of the people around here were moonshiners," Mickey said. "They made whiskey almost religiously, they took pride in it. This guy over here wanted to make it better than the other guy over yonder. They were a pretty independent bunch. They had to be, to live in these hills."

So independent, in fact, that when Alabama seceded from the Union in 1861, Winston County, which contains roughly half the Bankhead Forest, attempted to secede from Alabama. The people, mostly poor farmers, owned few slaves and had little sympathy for the Southern cause. Many fought for the Union, and the county became a refuge for others who refused to take up arms.

An earlier war, the American Revolution, divided the people of another southern state in what Professor Henry Lumpkin of the University of South Carolina told me was "a totally savage war of mutual extinction." The historian explained (Continued on page 56)

*G*iant and midgets of the swamp: A massive cypress rises from the mirrorlike
Little Pee Dee River in South Carolina. A green tree frog (far left) clings to a
vine-covered twig, and a tiny roseling—a variety of spiderwort—opens its
delicate blossoms. Stained to the color of strong tea by decaying vegetation, the
river meanders over the coastal plain through a forest of cypresses, tupelos,
birches, and willows that harbors deer and wild turkeys, alligators and waterfowl.

$\mathcal{H}$arvesttime in August sets the whole family to work on William L. Cook's tobacco farm beside the Little Pee Dee. He and his granddaughter Carla strip the leaves from the stalks, while Mrs. Cook drives a tractor pulling a trailer to collect the crop. Three generations of the family hurry along the rows to get the tobacco into the curing barn at its prime. Clothes dry on a line at a tenant farmer's house on one of the many farms that edge the river.

how, by inciting the Cherokee to attack the colonists and by failing to protect Tory sympathizers, the British engineered their own defeat. "Someone should erect a monument to the British generals who won the war for us," he said with the hint of a smile.

He went on to discuss a revolutionary figure whose name lives in South Carolina's and the nation's history, the legendary Francis Marion, the "Swamp Fox." Marion and his volunteers waged guerrilla warfare against the British in the Santee-Pee Dee country of cypress and tupelo swamps. Bill and I visited the Little Pee Dee, a black-water river nominated in 1980 for state protection as a scenic waterway, and found the country much as Marion must have known it.

The Pee Dee and its "Little" namesake might be much better known if Stephen Foster had not changed the original wording of his famous song to "Way down upon the Swanee River." Still, canoeists are becoming better acquainted with the Little Pee Dee, and it has always been popular with local fishermen. Its waters, stained by decaying vegetation, are about the color of strong tea, and though there are no rapids as such, the current runs powerful and swift. We paddled and drifted down several reaches, following the twisted course and braided channels in the cool, speckled shade of overhanging trees.

The upper half of the 108-mile-long river is fairly well populated; there are houses, summer camps, tobacco and soybean farms. The lower half is truly wild and, in my imagination, full of snakes. "There are no snakes," said Bill emphatically. "Anyway, there's nothing wrong with snakes, it's all a myth."

Sgt. Pearly E. Britt of the state's Wildlife and Marine Resources Department took me on a motorboat tour of the last section of the river. We went from the Great Pee Dee into the Little. Where the two met, I could see a definite line between the dark waters of the Little Pee Dee and the lighter mud-brown of the Great. Black and brown gradually blended a short distance downstream. Pearly spotted a snake basking on a fallen tree. "There's lots of snakes," he said. "Fishermen usually kill them because they eat up all the little fishes." We went searching for alligators—"Oh, there's plenty of them," Pearly had said—but after countless miles of swamp we gave up.

I didn't see an alligator until I went to the Peace, another black-water river that rises in Florida's lake country and empties into the Gulf of Mexico at Charlotte Harbor. It is one of Florida's longest rivers, and although it begins and ends near centers of population, it is one of the wildest. Bill couldn't join me this time, and I paddled the Peace with Julie Morris, a young environmentalist and co-author of a comprehensive report on the river. We launched her aluminum canoe near Bartow and immediately entered a sunless swamp where great bald cypresses thrust their bony knees out of the black-mirror water, and egrets and herons rattled the silence with their screeches.

In our first five-hour stretch we saw numbers of little blue, great blue, tricolored, and night herons, white ibises and great egrets, anhingas, red-winged blackbirds, barred owls—"Who cooks for yoooou?" Julie imitated their call—and a great horned owl. There were many ospreys, and I admired their elegant, well-shaped nests festooned with Spanish moss. (On Chesapeake Bay, where I sail in the summer, the ospreys build ungainly nests of driftwood and sticks.)

We passed under overhanging branches, called "sweepers," and I learned to duck low to avoid the enormous almost-cable-strength spider webs, the work of the golden orb weaver. Several times we heard loud splashes—turtles or alligators flopping into the river, disturbed by our passage. Once there was a huge splash right beside me that left me soaked. Julie thought it was a garfish, but later we decided it must have been an alligator just beneath the surface.

Below Arcadia the river began to widen, within more clearly defined banks. We saw increasing numbers of the little saw palmettos, cabbage palms, live oaks, stands of grass, and sandy beaches. Snow-white cattle egrets roamed among grazing livestock. Recent rains had swelled the river. Where we camped for the evening it had spilled into an old oxbow lake that was once its bed. We went for a cooling swim, and I could barely make headway against the strong current. Despite a threatening storm, we canoed into the lake among the cypresses, where we heard more turtle-or-alligator splashes.

When the storm broke, the rain turned the river into boiling silver, and we scurried back to camp, drenched. That night, long after dark, we heard voices. Peering from my tent I saw a boat with a light, drifting with the current. I called softly to Julie, and she whispered from her tent, "Frog hunters or alligator poachers." Later we heard shots; and, much later, the boat's engine as it returned upstream.

Next morning dawned sunny. Soon after we left the sandspit where we had camped under huge live oaks, we saw something swimming: an alligator! Only its snout, eyes, and the back of its head were visible, but from the size of the head Julie judged the reptile must have been 10 to 12 feet long. Unmindful, the gator passed us on a reciprocal course: it upstream, and we, very carefully, down.

The current had become so strong that often we simply drifted. When the sun got too hot, we would wedge the canoe among the knees of a cypress to cool off in its shade. By the end of our trip, the air had the tang of salt and the river had taken on the character of an estuary, although we were still many miles from Charlotte Harbor. We saw a sign warning motorboaters to be careful of manatees, and as we unloaded the canoe the river bade us goodbye with a volley of thunder and a cold lash of rain.

By now I had enjoyed a kaleidoscopic view of eight eastern rivers: only a small sampling, and yet enough to reveal each stream's individuality. Rivers are living things; more, they are wild living things—and, like wild plants and wild animals, are sometimes threatened by the conflicting needs of people in our populous East. Yet there is hope. Treated with a little kindness and a little thought, rivers can, and do, come back to life, even from the shadow of extinction.

FOLLOWING PAGES: On the grassy floodplain of Florida's Peace River, ranch hands round up a herd of cattle. Ranches along the Peace have kept the river wild against the pressures of developers and phosphate-mining interests.

A blazing
thunderbolt shatters the
glow of dawn over the
Peace into fleeting,
ominous glare. In
the approaching storm,
cabbage palms—
Florida's state tree—
stand silhouetted
against the burning
sky; on the riverbank, a
camper's tent promises
refuge from the
impending cloudburst.
Such summer
downpours usually
occur in late afternoon
and often send the river
over its low banks into
a maze of channels and
quiet backwaters that
shelter wildlife and
delight the water-borne
traveler.

Heartland treasure: The Niobrara River, core of a forested valley, winds below hundreds of miles of treeless Nebraska prairie. Late sun shades cottonwoods and cedars south of the river; beyond a wooded floodplain, ponderosa pines scale the north bank. Like the Niobrara, streams from Louisiana to Minnesota flow through history, past wilderness panoramas, and into adventure.

By Toni Eugene
Photographed by Matt Bradley

The
Heartland

America's rivers, once the pathways of Indians, explorers, and pioneers, now play hide-and-seek with highway bridges, wind through cities behind telltale lines of trees, or slow and defer to massive dams. For two months I explored such streams in our country's heartland. From airplanes and interstates many of them seem tame; but when I got my feet wet, I found that the rivers' magic still endures, and I shared the many pleasures of making a river a friend.

My travels began in the delta of southern Louisiana. Here the Mississippi River and its tributaries have deposited millions of tons of sediment annually and created a maze of swamps, marshes, and bayous. French Catholics, persecuted in the Canadian province of Acadia, came to this region in the 1750s to farm, trap, and fish. The French influence persists in the language, the cooking, and the music of their descendants—the Cajuns.

One of hundreds of delta streams, Bayou Penchant lies in the middle of Cajun country, only an hour's drive from New Orleans and just 20 miles from Morgan City, a major port for Louisiana's oil and gas fields. But Penchant is a world apart. It is a 30-mile-long strip of fresh-water marsh and peat-stained water that nourishes catfish, waterfowl, alligators, and nutria in flat wetlands of waving grass. Trappers and fishermen are the most frequent visitors.

Although oil and gas exploration has intensified throughout the Gulf of Mexico, Louisiana can restrict dredging and drilling in this bayou because it is one of 48 waterways in the state's Natural and Scenic Streams System. The state Department of Wildlife and Fisheries administers the scenic streams program; state biologists Kerry St. Pé, Mike Schurtz, and Kirk Cormier guided me in to Penchant in early May. Kerry is a Cajun himself, a fact evident from his surname and suggested by his wavy dark hair and soft, lilting speech. We stopped for picnic supplies at the combination general store and gas station that is most of the town of Gibson. C. J. Leger, a florid Cajun with a rumbling voice, runs the place, which stocks everything from hot sausages and thread to auto parts and four kinds of live worms. A sign outside promises bread "so fresh you may want to slap it."

A few miles west of Gibson, Kerry, Mike, and Kirk carefully backed their 20-foot powerboats into the dark waters of Bayou Black. Past lily pads bright with yellow blossoms, cypress trees and live oaks draped with Spanish moss, we sped toward Morgan City. In the Intracoastal Waterway our boats pounded against the wakes of supply ships on the way to and from drilling rigs in the Gulf. But when we turned left into Penchant, we were suddenly alone in a 400-foot-wide expanse of thick brown water lined with flatlands of tall grass and a few black willow trees.

At least, I thought we were alone. Then I noticed white blotches in some of the willows and made out the graceful shapes of ibises. Kerry pointed to a shaggy brown dot swimming rapidly toward shore. "A nutria," he said. I had been hoping for a close-up of these aquatic rodents. Introduced from Argentina in 1938, they are now more numerous in the marsh than the muskrats originally found here. Penchant, I saw at once, was packed with life. Tiny shad, alarmed by the propellers of our boats, exploded out of the water. On shore, a big white pelican turned to watch us, waddled forward a few steps, then flapped hard to lift itself into a graceful glide. Four wood ducks, heedless of our passing, bobbed in the swell like corks.

Kerry slowed the boat near a trapper's cabin to point out a narrow slash in the marsh. "That cut," he said, "is called a *trenasse*." Trappers dig trenasses—shallow ditches—into the marsh so they can take their boats in to set and check their lines. They often use small motorized "mud boats" nowadays, but pirogues—or Cajun canoes—are the traditional vessels. Kerry had brought a 14-foot boat handcrafted by his uncle. Pirogues float in water only a few inches deep. But they are very tippy. I clambered in gingerly, and immediately sat down as the pirogue rocked ominously. Kerry paddled stern. I sat in the bow and tried not to move a muscle. With every motion, the boat tipped and I cringed, but the ride was more than worth the worries.

In the silence two stilts, handsome black-and-white birds with long, skinny red legs, *neep-neeped* at each other. White morning glories and majestic blue flag iris edged the water beyond a field of maiden cane and senecio, its tall stems tipped by yellow flowers.

As we rounded a bend, I saw something moving. A family of nutria, five young ones with their parents, lumbered clumsily toward the water from their home on a pile of sticks and mud. These chunky, groundhog-size animals bore no resemblance to the glamorous fur coats I have always admired. The nutria's reddish brown outer hair is coarse and spiky. It is the thick, soft undercoat that furriers prize. Those pelts keep Louisiana leading the U. S. in annual wild fur production, and Penchant has one of the biggest nutria populations in the state. Paddling back to rejoin Mike and Kirk, I noticed more mounds; hundreds of them marked our way as we motored along.

Near the head of the bayou and Lake Penchant, the marsh is firmer and supports more trees. Mooring the boats at a ridge, we walked through thickets of bald cypress and tupelo. Mushy black goo oozed over the tops of my sneakers; leaves and vines grabbed my shirt. At Bog Island, a miniature swamp, we stopped for lunch. Spanish moss dripped from gnarled cypresses splotched with red lichens and green ones; misshapen cypress knees poked from murky water.

As we cruised back through the marsh, Kerry grabbed my arm and pointed to roiling water at a grassy bank. "Alligator—a big one," he yelled over the noise of the motor. The animal hurled itself from shore to seek refuge in its underwater den. Determined to see another one, I studied the shoreline through Kerry's binoculars. My reward came about ten minutes later. I heard splashing ahead and looked just in time to see a huge brown shape fling itself forward, churning the water with its powerful tail. According to Kerry, alligators are numerous in Bayou Penchant, and hunters are very successful here. Still on the federal list of endangered species elsewhere, the animal has recovered in southern Louisiana. The state has established a limited hunting season, setting a quota and allotting tags to landowners.

The Continental Land & Fur Company owns more than 60 percent of the thousands of acres of marsh along the bayou. For nearly 25 years Herman Crawford has managed that land. He told me that

Continental leases land to gator hunters as well as duck hunters and fur trappers. Mr. Crawford is a gigantic man, but gentle. "No reason to go out and start raising sand," he told me quietly. "Most people are pretty nice." A former trapper himself, he observed that trapping and fishing call for "some special people."

John Tabor is very special. He is thin, with faded blue eyes etched by laugh lines, and he approaches each day joyfully. For half an hour I sat on a wooden crate watching him and his brother expertly gut and skin 80 pounds of catfish they had caught that morning. John shared the fish fins with two cats and his philosophy with me. "You got to do a good day's work. If you're workin' for someone else, you work all day makin' him rich. It's better to work for yourself. I love to trap and fish—that's my line of work. The best thing about the bayou is I got everything there I want—the fishin' and the trappin'." For thirty years Penchant has been John's provider and companion. He knows each cabin and trenasse. But the bayou is not an easy conquest. Even by speedboat, I could only sample its treasures.

In south-central Texas I discovered a river that invites intimacy. The Guadalupe, rising in springs and flowing east 250 miles to the Gulf of Mexico, has cut a narrow valley through hills covered with live oak and cedar. Shallow, clear, and sprinkled liberally with rapids, it may well be the most popular recreational river in Texas. Tens of thousands of tubers and rafters jam the lower stretches on summer weekends, but above Canyon Dam the river is still unspoiled. Duncan Muckelroy, an avid canoeist, agreed to show me the Guadalupe he loves. This river lies in the heart of the Texas hill country, where live oaks line the highways, deer and roadrunners streak across traffic, and wild turkeys burst up from the shoulders. Pastures are so vast that cattle, goats, and sheep seem lost in them.

Late one afternoon we loaded Duncan's aluminum canoe with our supplies and put in near the town of Waring, about 40 miles north of San Antonio. The Guadalupe enfolded us—an avenue of rushing water 30 feet wide, fringed with centuries-old bald cypress trees. We had paddled only a few yards when we hit rapids. In the stern Duncan maneuvered the canoe; I paddled and prayed. These, though small, were my first rapids in years, and I thought back to my childhood canoeing lessons. "Read the V's," I remembered. A V pointing upstream indicates a rock or similar obstruction, because moving water parts at an obstacle. A V pointing downstream is usually the best course through a rapid, because it indicates a clear chute. Reassured by my recollections, I settled back to enjoy myself.

And the Guadalupe ensures enjoyment. Again and again we shot easy but exciting riffles and rapids. Punctuating the fast-water spells were quiet pools of clear green where minnows skittered. Cattle trails wound down hillsides to the river. (Continued on page 72)

Garlands of Spanish moss drape a bald cypress in Bayou Penchant, a 30-mile-long freshwater marsh in the Cajun country of Louisiana. Rich in dissolved nutrients, Penchant teems with waterfowl, alligators, nutria, and fish.

*Q*uiet as a country lane, the Guadalupe River slides between bald cypresses in central Texas. Above an empty clam shell, two snails cling to a root. Canoeists discover roller-coaster rides in other stretches of the river, where the clear, shallow water drops rapidly over limestone rocks and boulders.

PRECEDING PAGES: *Lacy fronds of a shield fern hug the twisted base of a cypress.*

Occasionally an ancient cypress with a circle of soil still clinging to its roots lay upended on the shore. Duncan explained that these giants were remnants left by a flood that ravaged the Guadalupe in 1978.

We portaged at one of several low bridges, then camped early on a rock-strewn bank. As night noises began, I watched fireflies winking like Christmas lights in a tall cypress. The sun went down red, staining the water; bright white stars immediately replaced it. Accompanied by chirruping crickets and hooting owls, the river murmured louder.

I woke to sunlight filtering through the cypress. We set off before 8 a.m. past sheer gray limestone bluffs dotted with cliff-swallow nests. Three black-and-white goats bleated plaintively at us and scrambled up a rocky cliff as we slid past. Beyond them stretched dry hillsides covered with juniper, yucca, and cactus. The day grew hot, so we stopped in the shade of a limestone overhang.

"Indians might have sheltered in this same spot," Duncan told me as we rested among bright ferns in the damp coolness. "Archaeological sites in this area prove man has been here for 12,000 years. In the late 1840s, when Germans came to settle this area, they had to fight Comanches and Apaches for it. Many of the ranches here now are owned by descendants of those Germans."

Too relaxed, we misjudged the current at the next rapid. Between a jumble of boulders and a fallen sycamore, the water seized us and hurled us against the tree. As the canoe began to fill, we leaped out. I grabbed the boat and dragged it to shore while Duncan sprinted down the bank after our gear. Running, wading, and swimming, he caught everything but my paddle. We emptied the canoe and went on more cautiously, still reveling in every rapid.

Cattle grazed in high pastures cradling the river. On one side Black Angus eyed us balefully; Herefords on the opposite bank looked much friendlier. More cypresses, snatched by the 63-foot waters of the '78 flood, lay in piles on the shore. At seven, when we took out, I asked Duncan how far we had come. "About 39 miles," he said. "Went quickly, didn't it?" It did. The Guadalupe is a fast friend.

Landowners along the upper river are not so outgoing. Determined to save this stretch from the fate of the overused lower section, they protect their interests fiercely. In the 1970s, when the Texas Parks and Wildlife Department proposed acquiring acreage along 22.5 miles of the river, local landowners quickly formed a protective organization—the Guadalupe River Association—and fought so hard that the state legislature finally scuttled the idea. When the federal government listed the Guadalupe for consideration as a wild and scenic river, the GRA managed to get it dropped from the list.

Pleasant but adamant, all the landowners I met insisted that they have been taking care of the Guadalupe for years and can do the job better than anyone else could. Some resent intruders; some tolerate them. Bruno Ranzau's German ancestors came to Texas in 1845. Now in his 80s, he was born and raised along the Guadalupe. "I'm divided," he said. "I like to see people have fun along the river. But some take advantage, lighting fires, littering, and even shooting game along the shore. We don't have any objections to people using the river as long as they obey the rules."

Bruno's neighbor Martin Marquardt allows camping on some of his property. But, he pointed out, "If you want to stay in the ranching business, you can't have folks coming in all the time. And ranchers need the river for watering their stock."

A 1,900-acre state park, opening in 1983 upstream from Canyon Dam, will offer camping facilities and public access to the river. Above that park canoeists can enjoy the rapids and the scenery, but will trespass if they leave the river without obtaining the landowner's permission. The GRA is powerful, untiring in efforts to keep the upper Guadalupe under private control.

*I*t's the federal government that regulates use of 44 miles of the Eleven Point River in southern Missouri, one of the eight streams originally designated in the Wild and Scenic Rivers Act of 1968. To maintain the character of the river, the U. S. Forest Service established a scenic zone—about a quarter-mile wide—on both sides of the Eleven Point. Today, the Eleven Point looks much as it did a hundred years ago; few buildings and highway bridges intrude as it winds through low pastures and forested valleys in the Ozark hills.

With Jim Roles, an assistant district ranger of Mark Twain National Forest, I spent a lazy afternoon canoeing from Thomasville to Cane Bluff. Twenty-four major springs feed the Eleven Point; this upper stretch, only thirty feet wide, is often too shallow for floating. The river gurgles over pebbles and gravel, meandering at leisure below gray limestone bluffs. Sycamores and river birches and box elders on both banks strain toward each other, creating a shady canopy.

As we set out in bright sunshine, watery reflections rippled on tree trunks near the water. Green herons flashed over the canoe; a small banded watersnake wriggled by. Paddling around a bend, we heard the beating of wings and watched blue herons rise from their rookery in a big sycamore. We counted 23 nests. Jim skillfully negotiated the riffles and pointed to limestone outcroppings where water splashed into the river from small springs. In several spots the darker green water of a spring branch churned up light brown sand as it rushed into the main channel. Herefords watering in midstream calmly stepped aside at the last minute so we could pass. Mooing drifted down to us. A fat old woodchuck started at our approach and scrambled into a grove of trees. All day we saw only three boats. In the last one a gray-haired couple shared the late afternoon in companionable silence. He fished. She worked at her needlepoint, with a big blue sunbonnet shading her face. Beyond them, red columbine dripped from crevices in a limestone cliff.

Most of Missouri's hundreds of springs issue from the limestone plateau and bluffs of the Ozarks. Greer Spring, which more than doubles the volume of the Eleven Point, has carved a deep-walled gorge through the soft gray rock. To reach it, I hiked a quarter of a mile down a natural stairway of tree roots. As I descended, the roar of water grew louder; you hear Greer long before you see it. Fed by an underground stream, the spring branch pours from a cave and builds momentum as it rushes downward over boulders. Another outlet in the bed of the gorge increases the flow to a torrent, and (Continued on page 78)

Rippling under an arch of birches, the Eleven Point River, one of eight streams designated in the Wild and Scenic Rivers Act of 1968, curves through green stillness in the Missouri Ozarks. Narrow and shallow here in its upper reaches, it widens and deepens as two dozen springs feed into it.

*S*unlight silvers the Eleven Point as canoeists paddle in a veil of mist near Turner's Mill, a landmark since the 1850s but closed and idle since the 1930s. Pockets of haze, formed when warm air meets the cold water at springs, sometimes dot the river in late afternoon. Five miles upstream at Greer Crossing, lawyer Charles Hapke from the St. Louis area puts business before pleasure; waiting to begin a fishing trip with three friends, he studies the financial news. The small launching site at Greer, busiest on the river, attracts hundreds of tourists on spring weekends and holidays.

the stream, carrying 220 million gallons of water a day, thunders toward the Eleven Point.

Below Greer the river widens and deepens. Shelby Smith, a soft-spoken fisherman with a wide, smiling mouth, knows this stretch well and agreed to take me exploring in a johnboat. Shelby, like many fishermen, prefers the stability and ease of a flat-bottomed johnboat to a canoe. The motor hummed, and water slapped the bow as we set out from Greer Crossing. Near an overgrown graveyard, wild watercress ten inches high grew in the cold water of another spring branch. At Mary Decker Shoal, the largest rapids on the Eleven Point, Shelby deftly slipped the boat through a chute. He lived here as a boy, and pointed out a big flat rock where his mother did the wash.

Beyond our johnboat sunlight flashed on a canoeist's paddle, and the river curved sharply around a horseshoe bend. White butterflies with black lacework wings chased each other through lush watercress at another spring. Shelby gestured at the banks as the river widened above the town of Riverton. "All this land was farmed when I was a boy," he said. "It's changed in the last twenty years. The government came in and took all the land along the river."

*L*ike Shelby, many long-term residents regret that the Eleven Point ever became a wild and scenic river. Some resent losing land; others hate the weekend crowds. Early on a Saturday, I joined the masses at Greer Crossing, one of several public-access facilities. Between 8 and 10 a.m. more than a hundred canoes were launched—one or two at a time—from the small landing. Trucks and cars clogged a narrow drive to the boat ramp; a few local fishermen with johnboats fought the tide of canoeists. Forest Service employees kept the situation under control. Many people, I thought, took longer to get onto the water than they would spend canoeing. The scene was a madhouse, a far cry from my serene weekday outings. Yet those Saturday floaters and I had something in common: gratitude that the Eleven Point has been set aside for our enjoyment.

Buford B. Morgan is pleased with the river too. A compact gentleman in his 60s with a precisely clipped mustache and a courtly manner, "B. B." Morgan owned a moss ranch on the Eleven Point for 28 years. He lived on the lower river at the Narrows, where a steep bluff is laced with four big springs. His moss grew best at temperatures of 50 to 60°F, and it thrived in the cold, mineral-rich spring water. Twice a week B. B. harvested the plants, packed them, and shipped them to aquariums from coast to coast. "We could have lost the river," he told me. "The Corps of Engineers was planning to build a flood-control dam on it that would have backed up the water and drowned all the springs for twenty miles. My springs would have been under forty feet of water. Making the Eleven Point a wild and scenic river is the best course we could have taken to preserve it."

Landowners near a 47-mile strip of the Niobrara River in northern Nebraska seek wild and scenic status to protect that waterway. The Niobrara was one of the original 72 streams studied before the passage of the Wild and Scenic Rivers Act, and it qualified for inclusion in the system. But a dam, part of a controversial and expensive irrigation project, was planned for the river. Congress authorized construction of the dam in 1972; residents continue to fight it.

From its source in eastern Wyoming, the Niobrara flows through 450 miles of prairie to join the Missouri River. Shallow and less than three feet wide in western Nebraska, the river grows as it collects groundwater from the Sand Hills. Mounds and ridges of sand held in place by tough prairie grasses, these hills are the most extensive dune system in the Western Hemisphere. They cover 19,000 square miles— about a quarter of the state. This whole area stores water. Rain sinks through the porous sand to the impermeable layer of clay that underlies the Sand Hills, and the water oozes out in low meadows, marshes, springs, and thousands of small lakes.

The Sand Hills flank the Niobrara above the town of Valentine, and the wooded river canyon is a narrow green ribbon in a sea of grass. Pines climb the canyon wall and cottonwoods reach to the water's edge. Canoeing one afternoon, I saw animals, not people. A golden eagle soared from a bluff 400 feet high, and a beaver waddled along the bank. At a narrow bend, a wild turkey, its tail feathers spread, flew up. Its landing on the opposite shore set off a chain reaction; a great blue heron flapped upward, disturbing a pair of mallards.

By the time it reaches Valentine, the Niobrara is more than 200 feet wide, a valuable source of water in a state where agriculture dominates the economy. Farmers in eastern Nebraska want that moisture for their crops; the dam near Valentine would give it to them. That same dam would flood 19 miles of the river. The Nature Conservancy, a private conservation organization founded in 1951, recently purchased 75 percent of the land that would be flooded.

Ben Brown, manager of the Conservancy's Niobrara Valley Preserve, told me that the 40 river miles below Valentine are unique because they are a biological crossroads. Here, where plants and animals live beyond their normal ranges, east meets west. "It's the most incredible area I've ever seen," Ben said. "The ecological diversity is tremendous." Here the north side of the river is dry. The soil does not hold water, and rain runs off quickly, carving deep gashes. Western forests of ponderosa pine and cedar cling to steep, eroded canyons.

Near white spikes of blooming yucca, Ben and I stood on a high bluff on the north bank and looked south across the Niobrara. Drainage from the Sand Hills forms springs, natural irrigation for the south side of the river. There the floodplain, a green strip of meadow bordered by cottonwoods and willows, rises to eastern deciduous forests of bur oak, ash, black walnut, and linden. Trees reach to the top of the river canyon; beyond them, sandhill prairie rolls in waves to the horizon. Because the plant communities overlap, animals also mix. Within two miles of the river, I saw western cactus and eastern tick clover, mule deer and whitetails, burrowing owls and Baltimore orioles.

Ancient glaciers reached south to the Niobrara. Paper birch and aspen have persisted here, and survive in the cool wet gullies cut by lesser streams. Shaded by a thick awning of heart-shaped linden leaves, I hiked in to a spring one afternoon. Columbine, ferns, and Canada violets grew on the riverbank. Honeysuckle tangled the grass. Through dense underbrush I followed (Continued on page 86)

*W*atery plumes from a sandhill spring plummet 67 feet at Smith Falls, highest waterfall in Nebraska, then flow into the Niobrara. Northern plants survive in the spring canyons. Paper birches frame the left of the falls; aspens climb a hillside. Eastern and western plants and animals also meet along the river. Red-tailed hawk chicks, almost ready to fly, huddle in their nest in a ponderosa pine. A white-tailed deer forages in tall grasses at Fort Niobrara National Wildlife Refuge.

FOLLOWING PAGES: Tubers rollick in the rapids at Rocky Ford, site of a natural rock dam across the Niobrara.

*G*olden bristles crown young spears of foxtail barley (right), a grass of the
Niobrara floodplain and lowland meadows. Common throughout the Great
Plains, foxtail barley reaches heights of two feet. Wild flowers light
the banks of the river; a vibrant prairie rose—about an inch wide—blooms
above a darker bud. "The Niobrara is a beautiful surprise," says the author.
"It hides below rolling, grass-covered hills. I drove north more than a hundred
miles to reach the river and saw only a few trees. As I descended a hill,
I suddenly came upon a ribbon of bright green—the tree-lined Niobrara."

a clear trickle to an eroded amphitheater of rock covered with moss and ringed by a dozen slender white birches. North joins east and west only along the 40-mile stretch of river. To an ecologist like Ben, "this area is a national treasure."

Thousands of canoeists share his opinion. One of the most popular float trips in the Great Plains starts outside Valentine, where photographer Matt Bradley and I began a two-day voyage. For five miles, the river flows through the grassland and wooded breaks of the Fort Niobrara Wildlife Refuge, which maintains herds of bison, elk, and longhorn cattle. On the south side, springs emerge from the Sand Hills as waterfalls. We beached the canoe and hiked in past paper birches to see the first cascade, Fort Falls—a glistening chute that widens as it plunges 30 feet from a narrow lip of rock.

Below it the river's current increased, and we passed several smaller falls plummeting into the main stream. Sunbathers on inner tubes waved as we paddled by. Like them, we drifted for a while—past a gray tree trunk overgrown with pink wild roses. Bisque-colored cliffs on the north and a red bluff on the south hemmed the river. As evening approached, we heard laughter and looked ahead to see a woman and two children riding a metal cage suspended over the water. The county built this cable car to take Fred Krzyzanowski's daughter to the schoolbus; he has lived near Smith Falls, the highest waterfall in Nebraska, for more than 40 years. We set up our tents in his pasture, then followed the roar of the falls about a quarter of a mile up a slippery trail. From a V-shaped stone ridge at the head of the spring canyon, water like liquid silver crashes 67 feet down into a mossy pool, then tumbles toward the Niobrara.

Mr. Krzyzanowski is 83, but he still welcomes visitors in person. "I bought this place for $3,000 down and worked hard to keep it. You won't find anything like this left in all of Nebraska." His pale blue eyes darkened when I asked him about the dam. "We'd be trading some damn pretty land for a sandbar." Behind him birch trees glistened in the twilight.

A few clouds accompanied us the next morning, and fluffy cottonwood seeds blew across the bow like snowflakes. The river dropped in a series of small choppy rapids, then forked around Fritz's Island. Fritz Brandenburg came to the Niobrara during the Dust Bowl days of the 1930s. His farm faces the island that is named for him. "This used to be the community swimming hole," he told me. In 1980 an ice jam blocked the left fork, forcing the river to the right of the island, where it churns and foams. Most canoeists portage here, as Matt and I did. Some try the right. From Fritz's backyard, we watched the whirling water snatch and swamp two canoes. "It gets pretty interestin'," said Fritz. "But there'll be forty feet of water right where we're standin' if the dam goes in."

Several miles downstream, the Niobrara boils over a natural quartz-and-sandstone dam at Rocky Ford, creating a torrent of white water that is one of the most popular spots on the river. It too would be underwater. Matt and I portaged the rapids. Below them, the stream grows wider and shallower and slower, braiding around sandbars.

One Sunday afternoon I returned to Rocky Ford and counted 250 canoes taking out above the rapids. Some canoeists pulled up with great style, turning to shore and coming in smartly parallel. Others, swinging their paddles wildly, fumbled toward the bank only to run aground in the sand four feet from the landing. At the rapids, tubers hooting with laughter rode the waves and chutes for hours.

Since prehistoric times, animals have roamed through the Niobrara Valley. In recent winters residents have counted 190 bald eagles feeding along the river, and the area is on the migration route of the whooping crane. Kenneth Emry, a wiry rancher in his late 60s with a sun-browned face and a strong jaw, remembers going home from school and seeing hundreds of whoopers feeding at the river. Near Rocky Ford, one of Mr. Emry's sons discovered the fossil remains of an earlier inhabitant—a three-toed horse.

Some of the most spectacular paleontological finds in the United States have been made on the Niobrara. Morris Skinner, born and raised in the Sand Hills, began bone-hunting as a young man. For nearly fifty years he collected specimens for the American Museum of Natural History. Now 76, Morris is short and round, with a trim white mustache and a pronounced limp. He took Matt and me to one of his most productive digs, at a tributary of the Niobrara where he has found more than 600 fossils. Armed with shovels for digging and balance, we inched our way up a 200-foot sand slide on Plum Creek. Morris advised caution; sections of the bank cave in without warning. "This is where I got my game leg," he said, indicating the stream far below us. "I landed down there."

Above us Matt yelled triumphantly and waved a fossil two feet long. He had found part of the tibia of a rhinoceros—a legacy from 11 million years ago, when Nebraska had a subtropical climate. I poked in the soft sand, finding nothing, while Matt unearthed pieces of a camel. "You'll find something," Morris promised. He showed me that the bank was composed of different-colored bands of sediment, and pointed to a reddish line. "That clay is part of the ancient riverbed. Look for dips and low spots in it where objects might have been deposited, then dig out the sand to the hard layer. Fossils are a different color than the matrix; finding them is largely a matter of differentiating colors." I retraced my steps carefully, probing with my shovel. Before we left, I had uncovered several prizes. Age has blued the enamel of my favorite, the molar of an ancient horse.

Indians used the Niobrara as a highway and watering hole for centuries, but ranchers did not settle in the valley until the 1870s. When blizzards drove their cattle south into the Sand Hills, the newcomers discovered the rich pastures there. They learned quickly that the prairie grasses were tough and durable—adapted to flourish in sand and to withstand Nebraska's high winds, blazing summers, and severe winters. They also found that disturbing this grass cover invited blowing sand and spreading dunes. Farmers tried raising crops, but coarse soils and drought defeated them. Ranchers succeeded; their cattle thrived on some of the richest grazing in North America.

The grandson of a homesteader, Philip Otto Rosfeld grew up on the western Nebraska prairie. For him, church picnics on the tree-

Trees and clouds compete with their own reflections on the glassy surface of the Black River in Wisconsin dairy country. Curling past sandy bluffs and small, wooded valleys, the Black joins the Mississippi at La Crosse.

shaded banks of the Niobrara were welcome respites from weeks of labor in miles of waving grass. His arms are still muscled and his hands still callused from working on his own place near Valentine, but he also teaches music now—and writes ballads of the Sand Hills. I watched the river curl under a bridge while Otto sang of childhood—of blizzard winters, hay harvests, and old Sand Hills men.

Humming one of his songs, I followed the river east, where it widens and slows as it leaves the Sand Hills. From an old railroad bridge, I saw the Niobrara meet the Missouri. The rivers are equal in size here: flat expanses of sluggish brown. But the Niobrara ends, while the Missouri carries prairie soil east to the Mississippi. I caught myself singing one of Otto's refrains: "Wild river, Niobrara, always run so free. . . ."

*W*isconsin's Black River feeds directly into the Mississippi. French traders paddled up the Black in the 1700s and named it—Rivière Noire—for its tannin-stained water. From its source in bogs and swamps, it winds through the dairy farms of west-central Wisconsin. It tumbles wildly through a narrow channel at first, dropping eight feet per mile. At the town of Black River Falls, it changes character dramatically and meanders gently down to join the Mississippi in the city of La Crosse. Wisconsin geologist Bruce Brown explained why. Above Black River Falls, the current rushes over a hard bed of ancient granite. Soft sandstone underlies the Black below the town, so the river widens and dawdles.

With John Larkin, a young businessman whose hobby is kayaking, I hiked in to see some of his favorite rapids. The streambed is a maze of huge gray boulders. Kayaking here, John told me, is a matter of timing because the Black is a river of extremes. Often it is too low to run. Where there is enough water to kayak, the rapids can quickly become Class IV or V. According to the international scale, Class V rapids are "extremely difficult, long and very violent . . . there is significant hazard to life in the event of a mishap."

A hydroelectric dam at Black River Falls obliterates the feature for which the town was named. Nearby, a French fur trader named Joseph Rolette established an Indian trading post in 1820. The federal government began transporting Wisconsin's Winnebago Indians to reservations farther west in the 1830s. But many came back. About seven miles east of Black River Falls live some of their descendants.

One of them, Eli Youngthunder, a powerfully built man with steel-gray hair, is a tribal elder. This Winnebago settlement, he said, was originally a mission of the German Reformed Church. The land, about 220 acres, now belongs to the Indians. "Indian Mission has changed a lot," Eli told me, "from wigwams to tar shacks to decent housing. But the river has been the same way as long as I can remember. You jumped in a canoe to go to La Crosse."

I paddled part of that 70-mile journey with Art Doll, a lanky and athletic employee of the Wisconsin Department of Natural Resources. Silver maple, birch, and pines shaded our put-in below Black River Falls. The water, about 200 feet wide, reflected the trees like a black mirror. This is the Driftless Area, the only part of Wisconsin unscarred by Ice Age glaciers. Eroded sand bluffs and narrow wooded valleys border the river; we paddled past hundreds of sandbars and a few other boats. Art and I agreed on a basic canoeing truth: If there is wind, it blows upstream—never down. All day we fought a stiff breeze.

Gusts tore at the canoe as we headed south from the landing at North Bend. The river, about three feet deep and 150 feet wide, glided past sandstone ledges draped with purple wild flowers. Old pine trees, their gnarled roots growing backward into the hillside, clung to the rock. Kingfishers started up at our approach. A clump of brilliant orange day lilies nodded in the wind, and the sweet smell of white elderberry blossoms wafted to the canoe. Birds sang to us while we ate lunch on a sandbar, and the sun weakly tried to burn off low clouds. The river slowed through flat bottomland as we neared the Mississippi; we took out about six miles above the confluence.

In the 1840s, steamboats brought settlers up the Mississippi and loggers discovered the wilderness along the Black. I learned about the logging boom in Black River Falls from Lawrence Jones, whose great-grandfather Jacob Spaulding completed a sawmill there in 1841. Tall and distinguished, with touches of white in his hair, Mr. Jones has lived in the town for all of his 86 years. "This country had huge, high-grade white pine," he told me. "Thousands of logs rode the river south to the Mississippi, then on to St. Louis." The forests were leveled, and the industry faded. Lawrence Jones saw the era end in 1905; he watched the last raft of lumber head down the Black.

*M*innesota, once 70 percent forest and much of that evergreen, attracted loggers too; the Big Fork River ferried timber to the Canadian border. The river rises in the lakes and marshes of north-central Minnesota and runs slowly east through swampland and beds of wild rice before turning north into dense woodlands of cedar, pine, spruce, and fir. Loggers began clearing those trees in the 1880s.

When the federal government made land available in 1900, settlers poured into the Big Fork valley. Howard Helm came in 1916, when few roads reached the river. He is almost 90, but still powerful. "I used to walk from my cabin to Bigfork to go to the bank," he told me. "That was 25 miles round trip. In spring and summer you could mire a duck in some of the mudholes, but in winter you could go anywhere because everything was frozen. That's when we logged. Sometimes it was 55° below zero." With the spring thaw, men floated the timber to Canada—a 135-mile run that took at least ten weeks.

The Big Fork carries canoeists now; it is one of 18 Canoe and Boating Routes maintained by the Minnesota Department of Natural Resources. Wilderness marks much of the river's 165-mile length. Only two towns intrude: Bigfork and Big Falls. The river was swollen with rain when Matt and I put in near Bigfork. Water the color of root beer flooded fields and pastures. The current, about four miles an hour, whisked us past houses and through groves of trees. We wound past a weathered barn high on a hillside; then, rounding a bend, saw the same building again. The forest closed in on us.

In the late afternoon we tied up near a stand of cedar to explore Klondike Landing, site of an old (Continued on page 96)

Swollen with spring rain, Minnesota's Big Fork River surges past a quartet of paper birches on its 165-mile trip to the Canadian border. Softwood logs by the thousand went down the Big Fork in the early 1900s; now the river floats canoeists and fishermen through remote north-woods wilderness.

*A*rtist and artisan, William Hafeman shapes ribs for a birchbark canoe in his workshop on the banks of the Big Fork. In sixty years Bill has mastered the ancient Chippewa method of building canoes out of birch bark. Now 84, he still combs the forests for suitable bark and completes five or six boats a year. "The Indians made canoes for life," he says. "A boat gets better every year. The bark shrinks, and it gets tighter and smoother." His hands enact the change (below, left) as he speaks. For ten years Bill fashioned canoes and gave them away; during the Depression, he made his first sale, for $25. Museums exhibit his creations now, and a finished 16-foot boat (below, right) sells for $925.

logging camp. For nearly an hour, a carpet of pine needles muffled our struggles as we squished across thick patches of moss and crawled over fallen trunks four feet in diameter. I reached out to steady myself on tree limbs; soft with decay, they disintegrated at my touch. We found no sign of the camp, and were glad to point the canoe downstream again. The river sped us to the highway bridge that marked our take-out, and we beached near four peeling birches.

I learned about birches from 84-year-old William Hafeman, a gaunt and tall, gray-haired man with a flowing handlebar mustache and large, expressive hands. More than 60 years ago, when Bill came to the Big Fork with his wife, Violet, he needed a boat to run his trap-lines along the river and learned the Chippewa method of crafting canoes from birchbark. "My first bark canoe didn't turn out very good," he confided. "It looked like a banana, and you had to keep your cigarette in the middle of your mouth or you'd roll over. But you improve all your life."

Now Bill's boats are works of art. He scours the woods for suitable trees and peels the bark himself. "A good birch wants to grow in a dense forest where there is no wind," he explained. "In the wind he bends and his bark splits." Holding the bow of a nearly completed 17-foot boat, Bill showed me how he uses split spruce roots to lash sheets of bark onto cedar gunwales, then installs cedar planking and ribs. "Bark is very strong," he said, smiling as I tried to tear a piece. "And there's nothing you can't repair on a birchbark canoe. The canoe was as important in the north as the covered wagon was in the west. The Indians would never have gotten into the woods without it. They needed something durable, but light enough to carry."

Two drops on the Big Fork demand portages. At Little American Falls, about 35 miles north of Bill Hafeman's Boat Works, the river plummets six feet over granite ledges and boulders. In a quarter-mile series of rapids and chutes near Big Falls, it plunges another 35 feet. From a park at the edge of town, I watched chocolate-brown water rage over granite, then boil up in ivory spray six feet high. Waves shouldered each other, colliding in fountains of foam. Uprooted trees cracked and split as they bounced against rocks in the channel. Far downstream, pillows of froth still flecked the water. Beyond Big Falls the river slows through winding miles of remote forest. I passed one small settlement, Lindford, on my way to the Big Fork's mouth at the Rainy River.

Five grassy hillocks, burial mounds of ancient Indians, dot the small tongue of marshland between the Big Fork and the Rainy. One of them, Grand Mound, is the largest in Minnesota. Archaeologists have named the builders—the Laurel—and determined that they constructed the mounds between 200 B.C. and A.D. 800. From an interpretive center that houses Laurel artifacts, I walked to the water's edge. The scene was the same two thousand years ago when the Laurel folk found a home by the rivers; at my feet the Rainy, joined by the Big Fork, churned westward.

A highland area that borders Lake Superior divides drainage: northward to Hudson Bay, eastward to the Great Lakes, and southward to the Mississippi River. The source of the Big Fork is less than a hundred miles from Lake Itasca, source of the Mississippi. South of the watershed, the Messipi—Great River—of the Chippewa Indians begins its 2,348-mile journey to the Gulf of Mexico. Its funnel-shaped drainage basin takes in 31 states: a web of water that once unlocked America's wilderness and still binds its heartland.

One of the westernmost streams in this web, the Clarks Fork of the Yellowstone, originates in the northeastern slopes of the Rockies. Fed by snowmelt in the Absaroka and Beartooth ranges, it makes a short loop through Wyoming before returning north to empty into the Yellowstone River. For 23 miles of that curve, the Clarks Fork runs amok, tearing its way through a deep and narrow canyon. Most of the gorge lies in the Shoshone National Forest. With district ranger Don Musso, Matt and I surveyed 21.5 miles of impossibly rugged terrain and terrifying white water—a proposed addition to the National Wild and Scenic Rivers System.

From the crossroads town of Clark, we drove to the north side of the lower canyon, a glacier-carved, U-shaped valley about half a mile wide, squeezed between 4,000-foot walls of granite and sedimentary rock. The river, heavy with late-spring runoff, foamed over boulders. Like Japanese bonsai, dwarfed and gnarled junipers clung to the dry shore. White yucca blossoms waved above the waxy yellow blooms of prickly pear cactus, and the air was thick with the tang of wild sage.

Before the road ended, Don turned his Ford Bronco onto a narrow switchback trail. The river shrank as we zigzagged forward, then backward, up a cliff. I saw a mountain goat, balanced comfortably on a crag. We climbed higher. There are 23 switchbacks in that track; I thought each would be our last. At the top we continued on foot for half a mile, scrambling between fir trees and over car-size boulders for a view of the river. The Clarks Fork lay partially hidden below overhanging ledges. From steep gorges in the opposite wall thundered two of its major tributaries, Sunlight and Dead Indian Creeks.

Later, on the south rim, Don pointed out a tree-lined cleft in the highlands. "That's Dead Indian Gulch," he said. "The Nez Perces escaped the U. S. Cavalry by retreating into the canyon, probably here at Dead Indian. Chief Joseph brought more than 400 Indians and a thousand horses down to the river, then out to Montana." The story of the Nez Perce retreat is a sad, and famous, one. Ordered to a reservation in Idaho in 1877, these people left eastern Oregon and fled in a desperate bid for freedom in Canada. Soldiers chased them every step for 1,700 miles and finally caught them 40 miles from the Canadian border. I studied the near-vertical cliff, silently applauding the stamina and skill of people who would dare to go down it on horseback.

On our left, the ragged, snowcapped Absarokas dominated the horizon; before us stretched the middle canyon. From the road, we hiked nearly three miles to its rim. From that distant vantage point the Clarks Fork was a quiet green thread.

For about eight miles in the middle canyon, the river writhes through a granite vise called The Box, dropping 400 feet per mile. Beyond a marshy field of blue lupine and hot-pink wild geraniums, we scrambled up to the edge of the slot. The canyon is narrow here—in some places just 600 feet from rim to rim, and the walls drop sheer. Fifteen hundred feet below us the river boiled with murderous force around boulders the size of houses.

In 1976 Dr. Kay Swanson, in a group of four kayakers, tried to run this canyon. He is an athletic G.P. who has pursued his hobby as far as Alaska. The Clarks Fork defeated him. "It's different from any river I've ever boated. It's more violent," he told me ruefully. "It squeezes down between rocks like water squirting out of a nozzle. In spots it's not more than ten feet wide. When we came to a falls between two cliffs, that finished us. We had to climb out up the side of the cliff. I was as weak as a cat!"

Clambering back to the road was enough to exhaust me, and I was delighted that we could drive to the 136-acre ranch on the upper canyon where we would spend the night. A cable car ferried us across the river to the Wright place, the only privately owned land in the 21.5 miles proposed for wild and scenic status. Forested slopes and gray granite peaks rise above its bright green pastures.

Next morning I rose early to talk with Randy Braten, who had managed the ranch for thirty years. His long spurs and high-heeled cowboy boots fit with the ease of fifty years' wear. "My daddy came here when he was seven," he said softly. "I've lived here all my life. This country's like a magnet. If you try to leave, it'll suck you right back." Randy has a knack for understatement. "Oh, I don't do much," he drawled. "Calving in February is the busiest time. Then we work around the clock. Only thing I know really is how to push a cow's fanny down a trail."

Seeing some of those trails, I gained a healthy respect for Randy and his brand of knowledge. Matt and I joined Don and his colleague Ed Weber for a horseback ride along the upper canyon. Winding gradually uphill, we followed the river for a couple of hours, then stopped for lunch on a wide bluff. The trail down to the river pitched past trees and through creeks. My horse, Raven, accelerated his pace on the descent; I jounced wildly. At the river, we turned around. Up again—up a switchback trail. Raven huffed and snorted. His sides heaved like an accordion. I dismounted and walked beside him. I huffed and snorted; my sides heaved. At the top, I realized Raven had conned me. He was fine, but I was so drained of energy I could barely remount.

Seeing the Clarks Fork Canyon is a struggle; knowing it is impossible. A savage force in a giant's landscape, the river demands respect. It does not invite friendship. The beauty of the Clarks Fork lies in its primitive wildness. It lacks the easy intimacy of the Guadalupe or the varied attractions of the Niobrara. In more subtle fashion, those rivers—my rivers, because I have made them mine by boating them—can be wild too. In a small boat—on the water—nature reasserts itself. The smallest riffle can spell disaster, and a single paper birch can recall the wilderness.

Churning waves carve gray granite on the Clarks Fork of the Yellowstone River in northern Wyoming. Raging down from the Rockies, the Clarks Fork chisels a canyon so spectacular that 21.5 river miles rate wild and scenic status.

*D*warfed by dark cliffs, the Clarks Fork sweeps past stands of Douglas fir and spruce in the upper canyon. Rangers Don Musso and Ed Weber, trail riding with the author and photographer, pinpoint their location on a topographic map.

oam-flecked torrents boil over boulders as big as cars in the middle canyon of the Clarks Fork (right)—an eight-mile-section called The Box. Roaring through a tight slot in cliffs towering to 1,200 feet, the river drops 400 feet per mile. High winds, funneled between 4,000-foot-high walls, scour the lower canyon—a glacier-carved valley about a half-mile wide. Plants die at Cyclone Bar (below), where 100-mile-an-hour gusts strip the soil. Elsewhere along the dry river bottom, yucca, cactus, and wind-hedged junipers clutch gravel-strewn banks. Beyond the canyon, the Clarks Fork slows; its once-roiled waters feed the Yellowstone, then the Missouri, and finally the Mississippi River.

*Great boulders churn the Dolores River into froth at Snaggletooth Rapid,
an obstacle course that drops 25 feet in a quarter of a mile. By late 1984, McPhee
Dam will divert much of this flow into a reservoir for irrigation. Rivers of the
Southwest, like the Dolores of Colorado, scour deep canyons in desert plateaus.*

*By Lawrence F. Mosher
Photographed by Richard A. Cooke III*

In Southwestern Canyons

*I*t always happened on the third day. This was as true for the Dolores and the Yampa—the Colorado's last major free-flowing tributary— as for the rugged Escalante, where we walked instead of floated. And when it happened, it always created that same magical combination of joy and excitement, release and serenity.

The third day is when you really know you are on the river. It is when you finally let go of wherever you came from to embrace this wondrous new place of laughing, loamy water, salmon-red sandstone, sage, juniper, and supremely brilliant light that distinguishes the deep-shadowed river canyons of the American Southwest.

To experience these rivers is to sink, literally, into this other world. It is to think in geologic time. It is to bear witness to other lifeways, other gods. It is, ultimately, to feel the river as more than a white-water exploit or wilderness adventure—as a passage into your own humanity.

There is a value to a free-flowing river that must be experienced to be fully understood. When a river is dammed, it loses its wild and unpredictable ways. We know the value in controlling a river, but we tend to forget the value of its untamed spirit. America is losing its free-flowing streams. But in visiting eight of the Southwest's most beautiful rivers, Rik Cooke and I encountered a new breed of river people who are struggling to protect this heritage.

Our sojourn begins on the upper Rio Grande near Taos, New Mexico. It is early June; the winter's snowpack has been subnormal, and the river's flow has already peaked. The lettuce farmers upstream in Colorado's San Luis Valley are taking more water. By the end of summer only shallows will be left here. Farther south, in Texas, silt will clog the bed of the country's second longest river.

We are standing near the John Dunn Bridge, the only river-level crossing within the entire 56-mile-long Rio Grande Gorge. The Río Grande del Norte—given its name by Spanish explorers from Mexico in the early 16th century—begins near the old mining town of Creede, Colorado, and ends 1,885 miles later in the Gulf of Mexico. Here, on the Taos Plateau, its waters long ago cut a deep trench through layers of basaltic lava to create one of the Southwest's most broodingly beautiful canyons.

The gorge begins its descent eight miles above the Colorado border. In 1968, 52 miles of it came under the protection of the Wild and Scenic Rivers Act. Along the 16-mile Taos Box run, great blocks of canyon wall have sheared off to sprinkle immense boulders about the channel. Now we face the result: a series of roaring rapids and crashing cataracts of Class III and IV difficulty that have made the Taos Box one of the great white-water challenges of the region.

Jim Stark, the young river ranger, gives us a cheerful send-off. He tells us the river is running at 1,950 cubic feet per second, down from the spring high of 3,000 cfs. Sometimes in previous years it has roared by here at 6,000, and anything over 5,000 cfs whisks a raft along at a double-time pace. Now there is less water because of increased crop irrigation upstream.

We are in the hands of Kathy Miller, who manages a river-running enterprise with her husband, Steve. Kathy, a lithe and beautiful brunette, confides that she was knocked out of the boat yesterday in a series of rapids called the Rock Garden. She managed to scramble right back in, she adds quickly.

We float the first few miles slowly. A light breeze ripples through a stand of apache-plume, its delicate white flowers sharply silhouetted by the riverbank's black basalt. A muskrat suddenly breaks water and scurries upstream. We gradually overtake a family of Canada geese with four goslings. On shore, a prairie dog ignores our quiet passage to take his lunch. Wildlife is unusually varied in the gorge, because access for humans is limited to one crossing and a few steep trails. Before we leave it, we'll see more cliff swallows than we can count, white-throated swifts, a great horned owl, turkey vultures, red-tailed hawks, several empty eagle's nests, some mergansers, and a pair of mountain bluebirds. Mule deer, elk, antelope, beaver, black bear, and mountain lion are here, but we'll see none of them.

Before we hit Ski Jump, the first major rapid, we pull in on the east bank at the stone ruins of a stagecoach lodge and bathhouse called Manby Hot Springs. The ruts of a wagon trail mark a crossing, La Bajada del Caballo, long since abandoned. We pause to soak in the hot, opaque water, still enclosed by rock walls but open now to the sky, and wonder about the travelers who refreshed themselves here.

After passing under the Rio Grande High Bridge, which is 650 feet above the water, the rapids begin to accelerate. Yellow Bank lifts our 13-foot boat high on a giant wave and then smoothly sends us skimming down in a surprisingly gentle thrust. I relax a little.

But the rapids are coming at us faster. They develop into an orchestral crescendo of falling-water cacophonies, and I feel engulfed by their fury. I hear Kathy warn us to hang on as we come up on Powerline, the blockbuster cataract where the river plunges 15 feet into a "hole" of roiling froth that can stand a raft on end. The trick is to "ferry" the raft left or right, between massive boulders, and keep the boat from flipping until the hole spits it out.

Kathy is standing up now, using her entire body to tug at the oars, and I see how easily a sudden lurch could fling her out of the raft and into the turbulence around us. Then we hit the hole, cutting it closer than intended, the raft bucking me up, up, and out, and I hold on to the safety line with all the tenacity I can muster. Did I tuck my notebook into a waterproof box? No matter.

Powerline's yawning hole sucks at us in hissing displeasure as we finally escape its grasp in a last, wrenching thrust of the oars. We are through and Kathy is chuckling. We take the rest of the rapids in quick succession: Pinball, Rock Garden, Enema, Cork Screw. They are tough technically, but anticlimactic. Five hours after starting, we reach the take-out at Taos Junction, exhausted, soaked, triumphant.

Not everyone, however, gets through so handily. Among the boulders on the west bank at Powerline there is an aluminum mailbox that safeguards a journal. When river runners pause there to inspect the cataract and plot their route, they usually add their comments to what is now a lengthy narration in several volumes.

On June 17, 1970, one John McCandless offered this entry to show his respect for the mighty Rio Grande: (Continued on page 112)

In a dreamily quiet stretch of the upper Rio Grande gorge in northern New Mexico, a Canada goose takes flight. Above, juniper trees line the bank at Ute Mountain Run, just below the Colorado border, where outcroppings of black basalt give evidence of lava flows 3.5 to 4.5 million years ago. Above the gravel-strewn wall of the canyon rise the Sangre de Cristo Mountains.

"*Brute strength counts for less than knowing the river,*" *claims guide Kathy Miller, using all her know-how in the "Racecourse" of the upper Rio Grande. Left: Author Larry Mosher (behind Kathy) shows exhilaration at a big drop.*

"Today I am twenty-six and me and my kayak are portageing [sic] around this hellhole. And I hope as the days grow me older I have even more sense."

Nicely put, John. We understand.

Not far to the northeast, near the present-day town of Trinidad, Colorado, some 16th-century explorers showed less wisdom. Of the party, only one got home; the rest died without the last rites of their faith. Their countrymen named a river in their memory: El Río de las Animas Perdidas en Purgatorio, the River of Lost Souls in Purgatory. Today most residents just call it the "Picketwire," an Anglo mangling of a variant on the original Spanish. Few know its canyons of rich red sandstone, or the three-toed dinosaur tracks that still glisten in the river-bottom stone as if the giant reptiles had just trundled by.

The Purgatoire—it kept the spelling used by the French, longtime rivals of Spain for power west of the Mississippi—begins high in the Sangre de Cristo Mountains and flows some 150 miles northeast to the Arkansas River. It has never been thought of as a national treasure, like Colorado's Yampa or Utah's Green. But within its remoteness, beginning about 50 miles northeast of Trinidad, is a 30-mile section of blood-tinged sandstone canyon that has long been the personal treasure of the ranching families that own the land.

It's not easy to get at the Purgatoire's beauty spots. The river is runnable only part of the year, and because most of the adjoining land is privately held, few attempt it then. No paved roads come near it except a secondary route, about 20 miles from the scenic section.

Thanks to Willard Louden, however, and his battered four-wheel-drive Blazer, I got a bouncy but clear impression of the river from some of the spookiest rock-infested "roads" in the Southwest. Louden, a local rancher, gifted artist, and hardworking conservationist, has known the Purgatoire all his life. For years he has worked with the Denver public schools to help students learn "another value system appropriate to the wilderness."

"I see how fragile this is," Louden said one September morning as we looked out over the wide river bottom where the Chacuaco Canyon joins it from the south. "Aldo Leopold made the point forty years ago that man must learn to think like a mountain. Our very survival may depend on our ability to understand this complexity that surrounds us. We must learn to walk very gently on this land."

When we stopped at the Red Rock Ranch down in the valley it became clearer why Willard Louden was so concerned. The U. S. Army was acquiring 240,000 acres northwest of the river to use as a tank maneuvering area for Fort Carson. Louden had led the fight to block the purchase, arguing that the tanks would tear up the land and destroy the Purgatoire's secret charms.

Tiny Doherty, the widowed grande dame of the Red Rock Ranch, explained the local concern this way: "What I dread most is the dust. I lived in this country during the 1930s, and I know what dust can do. I have seen dust storms turn these beautiful rocks to a muddy, ugly gray." But she candidly admitted that she did not want to share the Purgatoire's glories. "I do not want the general public to see it; it's mine," she exclaimed. "Yes, that's it!"

Tiny Doherty won't lose her ranch, but I visited others on the northwest rim who would. Their impending loss saddened me, because they were losing a way of life, a home in dramatic beauty.

But if the Army does choke the Purgatoire and despoil its fragile ecosystem, those who love this river may suffer from a double irony. They knew that to open their river's treasure to too many people would destroy it. But by failing to share it enough, they lessened its chances to survive the increasing competition for water and land. Alone, they could not defend it.

That was an odd group, on the Yampa. Three were part-time sheriff's deputies from central Florida. Two were nurses from the Boston suburbs. One was an advertising executive from Los Angeles. Another was a Detroit chauffeur. In all, there were 18 of them, and halfway down the river Bruce Fitch, their 29-year-old leader, was ready to wash his hands of the whole crew.

This was a Colorado Outward Bound School rafting trip down one of the country's most exquisite free-flowing rivers. I joined it at Deerlodge Park, at the eastern entrance to Dinosaur National Monument. From there we floated, paddled, and splashed our way 70 miles to the take-out below Island Park in Utah. It was a five-day adventure in wilderness appreciation that Outward Bound conducts for all ages. I loved it, but suspected early that this time Fitch might not.

The reason was the attitude of the "good ole boys" from Florida. They did not seem to appreciate Outward Bound's goal of helping adults "renew their commitment to learn, to risk and to grow," stated in its brochures. They joked about the nature walks, ignored the group discussions, and on Fitch's birthday they threw him in the river. In one sense, however, they were already attuned to the spirit of untamed streams. As Mike Young, another river runner on the Yampa, puts it: "Here you don't take orders except from the river. It is bigger than you are, and that makes this a wonderfully humbling experience." Fitch would use the river's wisdom to win over his rebels.

We had four boats, each with an Outward Bound instructor. I rode in Fitch's raft, which also contained the Florida posse's ringleader. On the first day, one of the nurses fell overboard.

All of us learned more than we had bargained for, one way or another. For example, there were the phenomena called cryptogams. They were not, as I had thought, a spy's specialty from the world of James Bond. We encountered them en masse during hikes in side canyons high above the river, amid the Yampa's great white Weber sandstone and the red Morgan formation laid down 300 million years ago.

The cryptogams brooded black and crusty across the upper canyon's rock, spore-producing plants that mark a beginning cycle of life. We followed one another's footsteps across their bleak fields to crush as few as possible. Patiently Fitch explained that these lichens take fifty or a hundred years to grow into a community measured by the yard or the acre. Eventually they capture soil enough to feed the piñon and juniper seeds that blow among the rocks.

Also, we learned the value of driftwood. The Yampa had a lot, because it was undammed. Campers could *(Continued on page 118)*

*P*rivate domains along remote canyons of southeastern Colorado's Purgatoire River shelter abundant wildlife. A yearling pronghorn, rescued by the owner of Red Rock Ranch after an injury and allowed to roam free, befriended photographer Rik Cooke. Of a normally wary species, this animal stood still for a scratch and pat on the head. Near the ranch house wild turkeys search placidly for seeds or insects. Blending with surrounding tumbleweed, buffalo grass, and blue gamma grass, an alert roadrunner pauses for an instant.

After a late afternoon storm, sunlight warms Entrada sandstone cliffs more than 136 million years old above the Purgatoire River at Red Rock Ranch. The isolation that has protected Indian petroglyphs in such bluffs and dinosaur tracks in the gorge may disappear as the U. S. Army buys land for maneuvers.

use it for firewood instead of "downtimber," and leave the fallen trees to help build the soil. This is especially important in dry climates where materials decompose slowly.

One of the signs of a dammed river is the absence of driftwood. I found friends of the Yampa concerned over plans to dam the upper river at two places. The Colorado-Ute Electric Association, already able to meet foreseeable demand for power, withdrew its support for the project in 1982. But the long-term threat of damming continues.

On the last morning we nested the rafts to float through Island Park and share breakfast. We had all survived Warm Springs Rapid, the Yampa's scariest cataract, in good style. Even the Florida fellows had finally embraced a little of the Outward Bound spirit. At the last campfire, Fitch had confessed, "At the beginning I was very concerned," and they had declared, "We've learned things here that we will take home with us." It was for Mary Ellen McNally, however, the diminutive nurse who fell overboard the first day, to sum up everyone's feelings. She read a poem she had composed, which ended this way: "We are in the hands of each other, / And in the palm of the river. . . . / We have met the river, and she has accepted us."

A snippet of doggerel sums up a piquant story from another valley: "Her picks are rust / Her bones are dust / It's forty years / Since she went bust." If rivers could talk, this sweet alpine stream could reveal volumes about the foolishness of man. She flows just 40 miles from her origins high in Colorado's Sierra Madre to her union with the North Platte in Wyoming. But oh my, what this beauteous and forgiving lady of the Rockies has seen!

The Encampment River has a role of her own in the history of the West. At the turn of the century, the Grand Encampment, as her namesake town was called, grew giddy over visions of an abundant future. Its tickets to glory were copper for the factories of the East and timber ties for the expanding Union Pacific Railroad. From 1897 to 1908, Grand Encampment boomed. A local historian called its Rudefeha mine "the richest copper strike ever made in this country." On August 29, 1902, the *Grand Encampment Herald*, a full-throated weekly, described the logging "tie camps" upriver in heady terms: ". . . new territory is being brought in touch with the hub of progress, Grand Encampment."

The town, located where the river spills from the Sierra Madre onto Wyoming's high plain, swelled to more than 3,000. By 1902 a smelter had been built and an aerial tram brought the ore 16 miles across the Continental Divide in buckets that carried 700 pounds each. It was believed to be the longest tramway in the country. From the head of Cow Creek, on its route, journalist Grant Jones had reported its construction with euphoria:

"Whatever it is that is coming up Cow Creek the people up here have a new song, and they all sing it, and it is the happiest song that you ever heard, and they sing it while they work, and their hearts are light, and they keep in time with their picks . . . and their blasts of dynamite, and nature and man with a million voices in perfect harmony have converted Cow Creek into a veritable amphitheatre of song, and the name of the song is—The Tramway is coming, Hurrah, Hurrah!"

But by the end of 1908 the dream had died. Two devastating fires and a sudden drop in the price of copper closed smelter and mines for good. A long-needed railroad spur to the Union Pacific's main line, 45 miles north, came too late to save the district's industry.

Today Encampment—the Grand is gone—lingers on as a supply center for ranchers, hunters, and fishermen. Its population hovers around 700, and its main preoccupation is with its past. Residents have established a living "museum" of turn-of-the-century buildings.

The river is as dashingly beautiful as ever. She is the continuum of life here. If her waters no longer float railroad ties down to the town and drive the smelter's generators, no matter. The Grand Encampment's true and enduring resource still lives. And there are people here who look to her future with a quietly mounting determination to guard her wild and scenic virtues.

Ralph Platt is one. His grandfather homesteaded here, and now he is a grandfather himself. At 69, he still ranches, goes prospecting for minerals, and helps out with his son Ron's hunting and outfitting business. And on a drizzly July morning Ralph and Ron introduced me and my two daughters to their river's still-tempestuous beauty. From the outskirts of town we ascended the river on horseback, climbing 4,000 feet to the alpine headwaters deep in Colorado's Mount Zirkel Wilderness.

Along the way we saw Rocky Mountain bighorn sheep, mule deer and elk, and a parade of wild flowers that stretched everyone's memory. White yarrow and showy light-purple daisies were everywhere, along with clusters of lavender mountain penstemon and alpine aster, deep purple monkshood, and trumpet-shaped scarlet gilia. At the higher elevations we found Colorado's favorite, the blue columbine, and the unforgettable pinkish-purple elephant-heads.

Our ascent, from 7,300 feet to about 11,300, passed through four climatic zones. Soon after leaving the town, with its limber pine and juniper, we shifted from the plains to the foothills, where I admired the ponderosa pine. Just over the Colorado line we camped at Commissary Park, where we entered the montane zone. There Douglas fir gave way to lodgepole pine. Our destination was Encampment Meadows, well into the subalpine zone. At 10,000 feet we found the Engelmann spruce and the subalpine fir climbing the slopes which lead to Lake Diana, the snowcapped Sawtooth Range, and, finally, Mount Zirkel's 12,180-foot eminence.

The only road we encountered was a dirt lane that intersects the river at Hog Park, where the Forest Service maintains a station. Some 300 loggers lived there 80 years ago, and the remains of their small community are still visible. So are the six-foot-high tree stumps the cutters left standing, ugly reminders of a rapacious past.

Life at Hog Park was raucous, sometimes violent, according to the *Herald*. During the "tie drives" men occasionally fell into the river and died in the log jams. Many were Swedish immigrants. In a 1905 account of the fatal stabbing of Ole Martinson, the cause was stated as "a drunken row."

Grand Encampment once supported 16 saloons. During the

Fourth of July celebrations of 1903, the *Herald* reported, two noted desperadoes shot it out after a misunderstanding. "Owing to a poker chip getting into the muzzle of Missouri Jack's gun and splitting the charge, Red Nose Ike lost both ears while Missouri Jack received the full charge from Ike's gun." They dropped Jack's body down an old "prospect hole," hanged Ike "from the limb of a pine," and held a dance that "lasted until midnight, when all returned to their homes filled with patriotism and enthusiasm."

If Ralph and Ron Platt are any measure of the river's men of today, they are just as tough and a lot more caring about their lady's future. Most of the Encampment Valley lies in multiple-use national forest, and efforts to designate the river as wild and scenic or the land as wilderness have so far failed. Either classification would ban roads, which would be necessary for timber harvesting.

"Roads take away any sense of wilderness," Ralph said one sunny morning as we walked across the high meadow where we had camped for several days. The advancing sun had not yet dried the dew clinging to the tall elephant-heads flowers that flourished along the headwaters, and their shimmering blossoms filled me with gratitude for this glorious place. "A man still likes to get out and move around, and go into his thoughts," Ralph said. "We're almost over-roaded in this area now."

Ron Platt voiced another generation's viewpoint: "This type of country needs to be saved. I don't want masses of people charging in here just because it suddenly is listed as a beautiful place. But if everyone respects this country and treats it right, we can enjoy it forever without changing it much."

Before we left that sublime subalpine meadow, Ron introduced me to a final delight. It was a cup of fresh mountain-creek water from one of the river's tiny feeder streams. "It's the sweetest drink you'll ever taste," he quipped. "I call it my Rocky Mountain highball." And you know, I'm sure he was absolutely right.

*A*gony! One misstep and it was done. Down I fell, forward and toward my left shoulder, my heavy pack forestalling any attempt to regain balance. My right boot jammed between two rocks, and when I landed on my left side, I knew I was in trouble. Accidents should be avoided on Arizona's West Clear Creek, a stretch of incredibly wild canyon some 40 miles southeast of Flagstaff. Once you descend into this deep and narrow riverine gallery there is no escape for 23 miles. We were to spend five days clambering and swimming our way down this stretch, and it was midmorning of the second day when I sprained my right ankle.

Fortunately, it was that and nothing worse. Dave Garrison, the competent and cheerful paramedic who—thank goodness—had joined us, strapped my ankle as tightly as he could. He carried a UHF

To hike West Clear Creek, in north-central Arizona, "You're required to 'rock hop,' swim, stumble, slip, slide, and fall your way through," explains a forest ranger. Here, Larry Mosher steps carefully, having already sprained his ankle.

With no choice but to swim, floating their gear on inflatable mats, the author (in front), Dave Garrison, and Bronwyn James make their way in the dark water of West Clear Creek. In five days they covered 23 miles, lacking a trail to follow because flash floods from spring rain frequently rearrange rock piles.

walkie-talkie radio that could summon a medevac helicopter. But there was no way a helicopter could work its way down close enough to help in this canyon. My choice was simple: walk out.

Our able-bodied members were Dave, forest rangers Don Freeman and Bill Stafford, and Rik Cooke and his fiancée, Bronwyn James. The men took some of my gear to lighten my pack, and on we trekked, with me and my lame ankle usually bringing up the rear.

Only Don had been down this canyon before, nine years earlier. But his memory did us little good. The canyon had changed, he said, the result of too many spring runoffs that gouged ever new arrangements of boulders, downtimber, and riparian vegetation. We found the variety of trees exceptional. Below the canyon's 6,000-foot rim, with its juniper and piñon, grew Arizona alder and sycamore, ponderosa pine, ash, gambel oak, Arizona black walnut, and—rarely—Douglas fir. At times the canyon would narrow to less than 20 feet, and at its deepest would lie about 1,000 feet below the outermost rim.

The most distinctive features of the West Clear Creek, however, were its many pools, long and often deep. We had to swim most of them. We carried inflatable beach mats for our backpacks, and gradually we developed a system. Dave usually served as our point man, spotting the pools and scurrying back to tell us the best approaches and whether we needed to inflate the mats or not. Sometimes we could wade through, holding our packs above our heads. But that was risky; once Rik suddenly disappeared into a hole, dousing his sleeping bag. But his quick recovery kept it from becoming soaked.

For me the pools—we swam a total of 23—and the countless crisscrossings of the creek were a blessing. The constant immersions kept my ankle from swelling too much. And as we hopped, jumped, and careered down the canyon, it miraculously firmed up. On the fourth day I took back my full load. By the end of the trip I was almost back to my first day's rock-hopping friskiness.

Afterward, Dave, a native of Flagstaff, set West Clear Creek in perspective. Dave had rafted the Grand Canyon twice, but of this wondrous stream he said: "I've never seen more concentrated beauty in one canyon. Yes, there's a mystique about West Clear Creek because of its remoteness. But the variety down there is incredible. The experience was really intense for me."

I appreciated Dave's exuberance almost as much as his expert ankle-taping. Without both, I would not have enjoyed that rare Arizona canyon as much as I did. It's a swimmer's canyon.

Not so the Westwater. The Westwater of the Colorado River commands a special respect among those who are expert at running rapids. The first man to write about this treacherous canyon, a Denver mining engineer named Frank Kendrick, portaged 12 miles around its cataracts in 1889. (Maj. John Wesley Powell, who explored the Colorado in 1869, never saw this section, which was then called the Grand

Driblets of spring water seeping from the canyon wall, like teeth of a comb, 4, 8, and 12 feet long, spill into West Clear Creek. Rainbow and brown trout, sucker fish, and chubs hide in the many pools formed and reshaped by the creek.

River.) It was not until 1916 that two experienced Colorado rivermen, Ellsworth Kolb and Bert Loper, ran the Westwater in a cedar canoe.

Since then the Westwater has become one of the three top white-water reaches on the Colorado, along with the Grand Canyon in Arizona and Utah's Cataract Canyon. It begins in Utah, just west of the Colorado line, to drop 125 feet in 17 miles. The brilliant red sandstone of the Wingate formation looms more than 800 feet above the water as it thunders down rapids called Big Hammer, Surprise, and Skull.

Skull Rapid is the toughest. Just beyond its awe-inspiring hole, the river makes a sharp turn left. Over the centuries the water has scoured out a place called the Room of Doom, where a powerful whirl-pool eddies round and round, trapping anyone who fails to keep to the rapid's left. Once in the Room of Doom at high water, the only way out is up the canyon wall in a tortuous climb to the rim.

Sheri Griffith, part owner of a family river-running business out of Moab, Utah, took us down the Westwater when the flow was 6,000 cubic feet per second. This section normally peaks at about 20,000 cfs, but is considered most difficult to run at 17,000. Then it's at its boiling best, flushing out the canyon like a tidal wave. "There is no other river with the volume and drop of the Colorado," Sheri told Rik Cooke and me as we floated down Westwater before dawn one July morning. Rik wanted to "get the early light," and I wanted to see what the river was like so early in the day.

As we floated quietly downstream, looking for wildlife, Sheri broke out hot tea and "crumpets"—her term for store cookies—and we indulged in the satisfactions of our lonely daybreak river. "In Skull at high water you could park a van in it and never see it," she continued. "There're rapids here that can gobble up 18-foot boats and flip them. A voracious appetite—you sure want to hit them straight on."

Now the sun was spreading a golden glow on the river's satin surface. We floated in silence now, looking for beaver, muskrat, raccoon, and the great blue heron. When we saw the bird feeding on a fish by the sandy riverbank, it looked at first like a raven. The sun was behind us, and Sheri delicately ferried our raft toward the creature. Suddenly it seemed too big to be a raven, and as our craft stole up on him we exulted in our discovery: This bird was actually a golden eagle, still so intent on his meal he didn't notice us.

Slowly we floated to within ten feet of him. Then, abruptly, alerted to our presence, he grabbed a last morsel and strode off—indignation in his gait and bearing. Finally, stretching his seven-foot wingspan to the sky in a masterful ascent, the great eagle departed. We could not believe our luck. (Continued on page 134)

Wild watercress nourished by cool springs edges a stream that feeds into the Yampa River near its confluence with the Green at the Colorado-Utah border.

PRECEDING PAGES: *Past overhanging box elder and boldly striped Tiger Wall, rafts from an Outward Bound School glide down the Yampa. Manganese oxide deposits from water seepage coat the 150-foot cliff with desert varnish.*

Peaks of Colorado's Sawtooth Range loom beyond Encampment Meadows, lush grazing for livestock. In southern Wyoming the river hits Damnation Alley, called "a rock-peppered conundrum that puts kayakers to their mettle."

FOLLOWING PAGES: Bighorn rams rest watchfully above a clear-cut slope by the Encampment. Here, evergreen forests offer year-round habitat for wildlife.

131

The Westwater's aura of remoteness is one of its greatest attributes, and on that morning the river had yielded an unsuspected treasure—a close-up moment with this magnificent king of the western skies. Later we would come close to the great blue heron, too.

The next day we would dare the Skull and avoid the Room of Doom. There the massive foundation of billion-year-old black gneiss would shine resplendent in the sun, offering a rich contrast to the swirls of ruby-red aeolian sandstone above it. But the dawn's discovery back on the quiet water would remain the highlight of our visit to this wild canyon, so near to the works of man and yet by nature itself so strongly protected from them.

*H*ow curious his observations. How prophetic the vision. How haunting her name. She is El Río de Nuestra Señora de los Dolores, the River of Our Lady of Sorrows. She flows out of Colorado's San Juan Mountains to join the Colorado River in Utah some 200 miles away. But in a year or so she may be all but dead, the victim of progress, of technology, of political choice.

It was Father Silvestre Vélez de Escalante who first foresaw her destiny. On August 13, 1776, Escalante and Father Francisco Atanasio Domínguez followed the Dolores on their unsuccessful mission to find a route from Santa Fe to Monterey, in California. Of a meadow near today's village of Dolores, Escalante wrote in his journal: "Here there is everything that a good settlement needs . . . as regards irrigable lands, pasturage, timber, and firewood."

The expedition forded the river four times before turning northeast. In Summit Canyon, just below Slick Rock, the party tired of the difficult going and prayerfully cast lots to decide which of two Ute Indian trails to follow.

Escalante's vision for what became known as Montezuma Valley did not materialize for a century. In 1889, after placer gold and silver had been discovered in the upper Dolores and the San Miguel, homesteaders built a low diversion dam across the river. In this area only a few hundred feet of elevation separate the Dolores from the San Juan drainage, and Escalante's "irrigable lands" became a reality when a tunnel and "Great Cut" sliced through the divide to leave the Dolores free-flowing no more. In 1907 a second canal was dug, which completely drains the Dolores' scenic canyons by midsummer.

What promises to cripple the Dolores permanently, however, is a high earth dam scheduled for completion in 1984, about eight miles downstream from the diversion dam. The McPhee Dam, which is being built by the Interior Department's Bureau of Reclamation, will create a reservoir backing ten miles upstream toward the little town of Dolores. Then the river will no longer send its spring melt cascading north through its six vermilion sandstone canyons—except for a single period of regulated flow, probably in June.

Plans call for a minimum flow of 50 cfs below the dam in normal water years. For dry years a 20 cfs flow is promised. But the government has not always fulfilled its vows, and the Dolores' ardent river-running community is concerned. Efforts to protect the canyon sections under the Wild and Scenic Rivers Act have come to naught.

"The Dolores may soon become America's first Wild and Scenic Dry Gulch," writes Doug Wheat, in a new book called *The Floaters Guide to Colorado*. Wheat, who was the first kayaker to run the Encampment River, considers the McPhee Dam no less sinful than the Glen Canyon Dam, which choked one of the finest gorges. "Many conservationists wonder what is worse," Wheat concludes, "to flood beautiful canyons or to take away their life blood."

Local residents, however, support the dam. David D. Herrick, a veterinarian at the nearby town of Cortez, has run the river by raft seven times. He recognizes that white-water enthusiasts might have to wait three to four years—while the reservoir fills—before there will be water enough to allow rafting at all. Yet he wants the dam.

"You've got a resource that is flowing by now," he told me. With the dam, he says, the area under irrigation would double—to 61,660 acres, in wheat and pinto beans—and a marginal economy would survive, even flourish. Moreover, the dam could provide water for the Indians of the Ute Mountain Ute Tribe, whose claims to it have gone unmet for years: "We all agree they're entitled to it."

Their reservation lies 25 miles south of the future reservoir. They would use about 24 percent of its stored water. But the plan may yet founder on the cost they would have to pay for a pipeline.

Even so, the McPhee Dam gave urgency and sadness to my journey in 1982. There would probably be one more free-flowing spring runoff. And after that? Tom Klema, our soft-spoken river runner, hopes that rafting will still be possible, but when I asked about the dam he would just smile and look away. I stopped asking.

The Dolores is a river of many moods. On the hot June morning we put in, some 35 miles north of Cortez, she was flowing at around 1,400 cfs. She had peaked in April at more than 7,000. In another month she would be dry at Snaggletooth, her meanest rapid. For the first ten miles we ran through Ponderosa Gorge, the canyon at its wildest. Our 180-mile trip took ten days, and we had to portage at Snaggletooth because the water was already too low for safety.

Well into the third day I recognized that subtle transition from land to water. My cares from my life in Washington, D. C., dropped away. I watched the water and how it flowed, and lulled by its rhythms I relaxed. The differing personalities in the boats began to find their resonances with each other, and the magic of the river washed all of us with the power of its purpose.

Our Lady of Sorrows is, beyond all else, resolute. Over the millennia she has overcome the contortions of a growing land to run northward against the grain of geologic change. A series of anticlines slowly formed, buckling the earth's surface as the river cut through them to reveal strata going back more than 190 million years into the Triassic period. The dominant rock is the hard, vermilion Wingate formation. It usually lies several hundred feet thick, and is sometimes streaked with black "varnish," a manganese oxide.

The Dolores has cut great arcs through this superb crossbedded sandstone, sometimes undercutting it to carve protected amphitheaters. In some of these we found the ruins of ancient granaries built by the Anasazi, who lived in this region for about a thousand

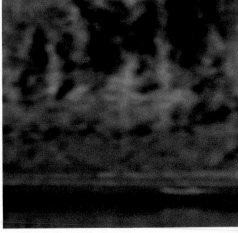

*I*nterrupted at breakfast, a golden
eagle stalks away into flight.
These majestic predators nest in
wilderness areas such as Westwater
Canyon of the Colorado River, just west
of the Colorado-Utah state line.
The upper canyon (above, right) cuts
through black rock 1.7 billion years old
—Precambrian schist and gneiss—
capped by domes and crossbeds of red
sandstone. Also common along the river,
a great blue heron skims over the
water, his gray body tinted by sunset.

years—or their neighbors the Fremont Indians. We also saw their rock art, mostly petroglyphs of animals with curved horns.

Occasionally the river would expose the Chinle shale, which also appears in Arizona's Painted Desert and Petrified Forest. Above the Wingate we saw the shelf-like reddish-purple Kayenta, the white Navajo sandstone, and the tough, darker Dakota sandstone, which caps many of the Southwest's mesas. These formations represent more than a hundred million years of climatic upheaval, when the region changed from sea to marsh to desert. It was the time of the dinosaur, of the earth's first birds, and of the first flowering plants.

The river seemed so sure of itself. I searched out an essay written by a pastor who had run Idaho's River of No Return: "Yesterday is always gone forever, a part of the river we have already run. Tomorrow is always unknown, a part of the river that lies ahead, around a bend, hidden by the towering walls of the canyon. But we do not fear." I did fear, though—for the Dolores. How was it that what had cut through two hundred million years of stone could be siphoned to virtual extinction in my lifetime?

This question has nagged the archaeologists upriver, who have been working feverishly since 1978 to unearth some 20 Anasazi villages before the McPhee Dam's reservoir covers them. The McPhee dig has become one of the country's biggest, and best financed. The money comes from the U. S. Treasury, which will pay for an Anasazi Heritage Center near Dolores to house all the artifacts rescued in time.

"At least these resources will get into the public domain," the dig's second-in-command, Allen E. Kane, told me when I visited the site. Kane praised the Bureau of Reclamation for its helpful attitude, and explained the significance of the McPhee villages. Their distinction lies not only in their size but also in their complexity.

"Their architecture was specialized," he explained, "such as the oversize structures they apparently used for holding ritual meetings concerning their food growing—to decide when to plant and harvest, and who would do the hunting. Some of these villages contained up to 500 people. In order to cope, they had to develop a certain level of social organization." During the ninth century A.D., in southwestern Colorado and northern New Mexico, the Anasazi tended to live in small groups; but here on the Dolores River they developed their largest communities. They grew corn, which needs at least 120 frost-free days a year; the area now averages only 90 days, and scholars theorize that a climatic change prompted them to go south or west. By the beginning of the tenth century, most had left.

The first white man born on the Dolores still lives. He is Rob Snyder, 83, and I found him on the river looking for one of his horses. I had returned to the Dolores in September to prowl its mountainous beginnings near Telluride. Rob Snyder lives south of Rico on his family's gold-mining claim, some 430 acres. The Snyders filed their claim in 1882, and acquired ownership in 1958.

"Are you Mr. Snyder?" I asked the white-bearded man leading two horses. "Yeah, what's left of him," he shot back with a toothy smile. He said he was born just north of Slick Rock, perhaps the prettiest of the six red-rock canyons I had floated through. His father had homesteaded at the mouth of Summit Canyon, where Escalante had stopped in 1776 to cast lots. The elder Snyder was one of the prospectors who mined a canary yellow uranium-bearing ore on the lower river in 1899; this carnotite was shipped to Marie and Pierre Curie in Paris, and figured in their discovery of radium.

It was the discovery of silver in 1879 that transformed the upper Dolores. Prospectors poured into the mountains to found Telluride, Rico (Rich, in Spanish), and Dunton. In 1893 silver prices collapsed, but the discovery of gold kept the area going for some decades. In recent years, all mining has slackened here.

Like many of pioneer stock who still live along the Dolores, Rob Snyder is only half nostalgic about the wilder past. He tells how some strangers stopped at a camp to talk with his father and a companion: "Said they were cattle buyers. After they had ridden on, my dad said, 'Those fellows are no cow buyers—they're gunmen.' Sure enough, it turned out they had just robbed the Telluride bank of $25,000—they were Butch Cassidy and his 'wild bunch.' "

Snyder appreciates progress, too. He thinks the McPhee Dam will add to the area's recreational worth, but dismisses its role in agriculture: "Most of those dry farmers who grow pinto beans won't want to pay for the sprinklers." And the river's value to him?

"It means my life," he said with a grin. "If I'd been a girl my mother would have named me Dolores." Then he showed me a small vial of gold nuggets he had recently panned from the river. "You used to be able to go out and dig a hole anywhere you wanted to go," he said, his eyes twinkling. "Nowadays, though, you have to put the dirt back in the hole, and then plant grass on it!"

We both laughed. On the upper river, at least, there is still that easy assurance which goes with confidence that the Dolores will always have water. For this river, that is worth more than gold.

"*T*he people who need signs and trails should not come here," Tom Gillette, the Park Service ranger, told us. "The Escalante's as close to real wilderness as I've ever seen." We had just spent nine days climbing—at times, inching—our way through the labyrinths of the Escalante's tortured canyons of white and pink-red sandstones. I considered Gillette a master of understatement.

The Escalante River was the last of the eight we saw. It meanders about 100 miles from its headwaters to Lake Powell and its now-submerged confluence with the Colorado River. Edson Alvey, of the town of Escalante, the river's resident expert, describes it as "one of the most crooked rivers of its kind in the world." One 35-mile section, he reports, travels a straight-line distance of only 14.

Seen from the air, the Escalante country resembles a huge, crumpled, sand-colored mud pie scorched by countless bakings. My fellow hikers Lucy Wallingford and Bret Blosser called the convoluted rockscape "the brain fields." Its pallid Navajo sandstone, which represents two hundred million years of the earth's history, inspired a member of one of Powell's survey parties to write in 1880: "Everything visible tells of ruin and decay. It is the extreme of desolation, the blankest solitude, a superlative desert." (Continued on page 144)

*H*igh above the Dolores River in western Colorado remnants of a hanging flume built in 1888-91 cling to the wall of Gateway Canyon. To supply water for large-scale placer mining, laborers constructed the flume by lowering men in rope baskets to chisel holes for support brackets. They completed 12 laborious miles—but the project never yielded gold enough for a profit.

To descend into the brain fields is to discover another world: of rainwater pools amidst the white, hot rocks; of eerie, narrow gulches; of river bottoms laden with cottonwoods, willows, the ubiquitous tamarisk and sudden patches of purple asters; of the constant, haunting, overpowering sting of silence. In Escalante country the wilderness experience transcends all past and future; every moment is a pearl of real time wrapped in an exquisite texture of sensory awareness. It is to be alive in all possible dimensions.

The compelling quality of the region seems to grow directly out of its hauntingly rich Indian heritage. Navajo Mountain's presence to the south suggests the theme that historian Karl W. Luckert has defined in *Navajo Mountain and Rainbow Bridge Religion:* "Without finding the proper balance between the human ego and its greater-than-human surroundings now and then, humankind would long ago have reverted to the level of brute predators. . . . Human cultures grow, as their individual builders do, with a measure of humility, love, and self-sacrifice."

The mysticism of the Escalante permeated our journey. In response, perhaps, Bret, Lucy, and I played a game of secrecy. They promised to show me their favorite haunts and to find new ones if I promised not to reveal exactly where they were. With our topographic maps always at hand (hanging from our necks in freezer bags), we set off one September afternoon to reconnoiter an area south of Death Hollow. Neither of my guides had explored this area, so we would all be covering new territory. We invented names for key places, such as an intersection of side canyons where we made our base camp. We called this Main and Center. From my log:

Sept. 20: Drove over the high desert east of town (Escalante); hiked about five miles to Main and Center, which holds a small pool. We fill our water bags. No signs of cattle, but we wonder about the upland drainage. They decline to use my water-purifier pills.

Lucy and Bret skilled at adapting health foods to the demands of wilderness cuisine. Tonight a "slow" dinner of curried wheatberries and rice seasoned with ginger and almonds, together with fresh broccoli, onions, and Chinese cabbage; to drink—burgundy. Afterward, we discuss the problem of publicity. Bret says Edward Abbey's book *Slickrock*, which he wrote to protect this area from highway development, has an ironic result. Because Abbey mentioned a particularly beautiful side canyon called Coyote Gulch, backpackers have begun to erode its wilderness value through overuse.

Sept. 21: We breakfast on a chewy homemade cereal—flakes made with raw oats, rye and wheat, shaved coconut, sesame seeds, cashews, sunflower seeds, bran, and cinnamon and raisins, which we mix with date sugar and powdered milk. Day begins refreshingly cool. Head toward the Escalante, reaching a promontory over the river. Bret scouts a route down the slickrock, but we go south to find a "big, blue pothole" on the map. It turns out to be not so big, but OK for a cooling swim. Lunch is pita bread filled with guacamole, bean sprouts, cheese, raw carrots. Set out to find "Little Cathedral in the Desert," named by photographer Gordon Anderson. Reach a breathtaking overlook of the Escalante—300 feet straight down. Return to Main and Center in the dark to cook spaghetti with pesto and okra from Bret's garden in Moab. The okra is too old and stringy.

Sept. 22: We head for the river again, this time to reach Little Cathedral at river level. Use a dead box elder to negotiate a descent down a narrow gully. I name the top of the slickrock "Uptown" and Bret calls the gully's bottom "Watercress Pass" because of the cress growing around a spring. We watch the blue and gray dragonflies, speculate about their courtship. Swim in the Escalante and note the giant patterns made by the lichens on the red sandstone canyon walls. Bret talks about running the Escalante, which was complicated by the construction of Glen Canyon Dam. Now you have to paddle five miles on Lake Powell to a take-out at Hole-in-the-Rock, or negotiate a difficult three-mile climb out of the canyon at Forty Mile Ridge.

Reach Little Cathedral late in the afternoon, a gallery the length of a football field, filled with cottonwoods. We find a huge embankment of ferns growing under an overhang that extends 40 feet out from the canyon wall—a deep pocket of perpetual shadow. Saw nothing like this on other rivers. Return to base camp by moonlight. It's a different way to climb slickrock: You see less but gain more confidence.

Sept. 23: Ascend to brain fields up Center East. Lucy, who teaches art, stops to paint. Bret and I go back to Center West, a dark cavern of a canyon whose towering walls at times almost touch. Bret warns that a flash flood could trap and drown us, so we try to watch for clouds. Found the bones of a coyote, which had evidently fallen from the top. Spooky place—I'm glad to get out.

The Escalante's northern section is controlled by the Bureau of Land Management. Its southern half is part of the Glen Canyon National Recreation Area. Backpackers are advised to visit the Park Service ranger's office in Escalante to find areas to explore. "We make maps available," said Tom Gillette, "and I'll share my knowledge with those who are sensitive to the values of this area. We want people to learn to be gentle with this land, and to learn to leave only their footprints behind them."

Leaving the Escalante, I recalled what another young man had told me back on the Rio Grande, in June. Perhaps Tom Mottl, the Interior Department's river manager at Taos, best sums up why all of us should try to preserve these wild and scenic splendors.

"What is at stake," Mottl said, "is the loss of a unique experience that is open to anyone who chooses to float with the river down a canyon. People fall in love with rivers because a magical thing happens. Maybe it's the thrill of the rapids, or the canyon's beauty, or the early mornings and evenings in the moonlight, or the experiences with the other people on the trip. Whatever it is, the river generates a beautiful and mystical feeling. When you take this away, you take away some of life, too."

A frightened deer peers down a narrow gully whose normally clear stream his stamping hoofs have muddied. Along a tortuous route in south-central Utah, from the Aquarius Plateau to Lake Powell, the Escalante River creates a labyrinth of such gorges. The Anasazi, Indians who inhabited this region in the 11th through 13th centuries A.D., left rock art in abundance.
Below: An artist 1,500 years earlier probably left this moose petroglyph pecked into the dark patina of sandstone near the headwaters of the Escalante.

*I*mpenetrable, pristine still, the Escalante Basin inspired a geologist in 1880 to call it "the extreme of desolation, the blankest solitude, a superlative desert." Like other wild rivers of the Southwest, the Escalante meanders in its deeply entrenched canyon through two hundred million years of geologic history.

Evening mist transforms Idaho's Selway River into a fantasy world. With rivers that rush to the Pacific through rain forest and redwood groves, rivers that cut through Oregon's arid basalt center, streams tumbling out of the Sierra Nevada and the Rockies, America's Far West offers pristine waters where Justice William O. Douglas found it still "safe to kneel and drink deep."

By Jennifer C. Urquhart
Photographed by Steve Wall

To the
Northwest

"I think of rivers as the blood of the earth," my friend Rod Nash told me. We were on a rocky bank beside the swift, clear-green waters of the Tuolumne River. "Everything sort of ends up in the river, running to the sea. Time and again, continents have eroded down," he continued. "There is no force on this planet more powerful than water flowing over time. I sense this energy, when I am on a river. I sense being a part of this most ancient of processes."

I was on the first leg of a journey that would take me to six of the most unspoiled streams in the Northwest and California. They differ, I would find, but, in their ceaseless energy, each offers a perspective that surpasses human scale. I would savor their wild beauty. I would learn, too, how people of this region feel about their rivers.

On the way to California, my plane had crossed the snowcapped Sierra Nevada. I could see the San Joaquin Valley, a patchwork of fields greened by the waters of Sierra rivers. High-voltage towers, like long-legged giant insects, marched down the valley, carrying the power of the rivers' tumbling waters to cities and towns.

Photographer Steve Wall and I had made a rendezvous at Groveland, a small town in the Sierra gold-rush country, with Rod, a professor of environmental history, his wife, MaryAnne, and some of their friends. We would raft with them through the middle canyon of the Tuolumne, one of the most challenging stretches of white water in the West, with an average drop of 54 feet per mile.

"The wild young river . . . still singing the song of creation," naturalist John Muir had called the infant Tuolumne cascading off Mount Lyell in Yosemite National Park. The river cuts through alpine meadows and deep gorges. Then the Hetch Hetchy reservoir, formed by the O'Shaughnessy Dam, swallows it for a while. Hetch Hetchy has, since the 1920s, provided water and power for San Francisco. Some say it was defeat, in a bitter fight to stop that dam, that killed John Muir. Below the dam, in the middle canyon, the river comes to life again. It was to this deep-forest haven for boaters, fishermen, hunters, and hikers that I had come. Downstream, 158 miles from its exalted beginnings, its water spent for irrigation and virtually dried up in summer, the Tuolumne quietly merges with the San Joaquin.

The river was running high, as we learned at the Forest Service district office: more than 6,000 cubic feet per second. A long-time "river-rat," Rod had rafted the Tuolumne many times, and had been among the first to run Clavey Falls, the major rapid. Ray Ford, a high-school teacher from Santa Barbara, with nine years of rowing experience, would man the second boat.

The road became rutted and rocky as we wound farther into the steep canyon. Small waterfalls burst out of the lush green slopes. By June the terrain would be sere brown. At the river, the 16-foot rafts were quickly rigged, and we were off down the roiling waters. Boyish-faced, Rod had clamped on his head a felt hat that must have seen a hundred rivers. Ray, tall and blond, sported a jaunty new straw with a feathered band.

Cold water poured over us when we dropped into a rapid called Rock Garden. The back of the raft folded up—with me in it. "That was only a little one," Rod remarked later in camp.

Shooting stars zipped past satellites and planets as I drifted off to sleep. A car's lights crept along the opposite canyon wall. A horn honked. Tomorrow we would be beyond any roads. . . .

I awoke early to birds chirping, invisible in the manzanita brush. Soon we were on the river again. The Tuolumne never rests. We danced through rapid after rapid with names like Ram's Head, India, and Evangelist (where, I suppose, you get religion). We hit one large hole. The raft shuddered, as if to break apart. A great wave crashed over our heads. But then, slowly, the water-full boat groaned up out of the turmoil, with all of us, to our surprise, aboard.

At Clavey Falls the water was so high that we had to hop from rock to rock, through alders and willows, to get near enough to scout the rapid. The Tuolumne, a white fury here, squeezes between a granite wall and boulders dumped by its tributary the Clavey.

A huge rock Rod calls "the dragon" bared its jagged teeth in the middle. I breathed a sigh of relief when Rod decided to run the boats light. MaryAnne and I watched from a high rock. The boats started down, and the river enveloped them. We could see nothing. Mary-Anne grabbed my arm: *"Is that Rod's hat?"* It was only a piece of reddish wood floating by. And then the rafts emerged into sight.

At lunch, we relaxed. On the near-vertical slopes, pale spring grass shimmered like watered silk as a soft April breeze breathed through it. Digger pines and live oaks dotted the canyon, thicker on the cooler, north-facing walls. A red-tailed hawk paused, midair, on an updraft. Violet-green swallows skimmed the water, wings flashing like scissors.

Soon we were at Big Creek, to camp. The river, calmer and wider here, plays softer music, the brushing of snare drums, as a million rocks shift on the bottom.

Like Saturday's child, the Tuolumne works hard for a living. Half a dozen hydroelectric projects aim to make it work even harder. And if any go through, a proposal to designate the last free-flowing segments of the river as wild and scenic might well be put aside.

Waiting for us at Wards Ferry, our take-out, was a slender, bespectacled man wearing tennis shoes so river-worn they barely stayed on his feet. Bob Hackamack, a board member for the Tuolumne River Preservation Trust, has worked to protect the middle canyon since 1969. "The new projects are single purpose," he told me, "only for power generation. The river is already producing 78 percent of the total energy it can." On any river, he pointed out, the best dam sites are chosen first. "Here they're getting to sites six, seven, and eight." The fishermen would lose. So would others. "It's hard to mine under 400 feet of water. Cattle have an even harder time grazing."

I went down the valley to meet Ernest Geddes, general manager of the Turlock Irrigation District. "We don't need the dams for irrigation," he acknowledged, "but to meet power needs. Our business is to make money and sell power." I had learned from the trust, however, that the needs were only for peak summer demand and that the projected growth in energy use for the area had been greatly overestimated. He conceded that, if the projects went through, the water quality and fishing might deteriorate: no more drinking the cold, clear water

*T*wo faces of California's Tuolumne River: Steep granite walls squeeze the middle Tuolumne into rapids that invite skilled white-water enthusiasts. Downstream, dams detain the river before releasing it as a sedate stream where fishermen angle for bass, bluegill, and trout. The Wild and Scenic System aims to preserve fishery habitat as well as recreation opportunities.

right out of the river. "But if you're flying over, you wouldn't notice the difference."

Mrs. Enis Congelosi would notice. "Where are our children going to see a river flowing? Are they going to have to go to Africa or Alaska to actually *see* a river?" she asked. We sat in her cheery living room in the town of Tuolumne, discussing the conflicts that decide the fate of rivers in this region. Enis's father, like many Tuolumne settlers, came from Italy; her still-dark curly hair, her bright eyes, and her energy belie her nearly 70 years. She became concerned for the river after reading an article on how a dam destroyed the fishery on the Trinity River in northern California: "It sort of opened my eyes."

Enis resents the outside interests—San Francisco, and the valley irrigation districts—that since 1913 have held the rights to use the Tuolumne's water. The county's 36,500 would receive no benefit from the proposed projects.

In my travels I came across a 1957 water-use plan that proposed dams and reservoirs for nearly every stretch of moving water in California. "That gives you an idea," a friend remarked, "of the mentality people had back then—before the environmental awareness that came out of the '60s and '70s."

That mentality may be coming back. A 1978 law designed to conserve energy could threaten every free-flowing river in the country. Under the auspices of the Federal Energy Regulatory Commission, FERC, incentives are provided for small generating plants that use "renewable resources," including water. The number of applications for dam permits jumped from 76 in 1979 to 1,858 in 1981.

One official in a government office pointed at a desk piled high with permit requests awaiting his comment. "We're being FERC'd to death, and most of the time they just ignore what we say." The issue is one of definition. Is a free-flowing river a "renewable resource," if a dam would destroy its ecology and its very being as a river?

As the history of the Tuolumne gleams with the gold of the Mother Lode, the Carson River's past is tinged with the silver of the Comstock. I had crossed to the eastern slope of the Sierra Nevada to see the East Fork of the Carson. The scent of piñon and Jeffrey pine filled the crisp air. It was hard to picture these slopes denuded of trees, as they were in the late 1800s, to fuel the smelters and shore up the mines of the Comstock Lode. It was hard to imagine the East Fork—a lilting mountain stream—"filled with wood up to six feet deep," as one observer reported, "through a distance of four and a half miles."

Below the confluence of the East Fork and the West, the main stem of the Carson meanders across western Nevada. Irrigation canals draw off its water for pastures and fields, in green contrast to arid hills studded with juniper and sagebrush. Diminishing as it goes, the Carson turns north and east in a futile search for the sea. Then this "river to nowhere" simply disappears into the Carson Sink.

Markleeville, elevation 5,500 feet, was my base for outings in this country. The town is a comfortable clutter of frame buildings with steep-pitched roofs that shed many feet of snow a year. I wandered down the shady main street, where columbines grew in crevices in the sidewalk, and Elizabeth Coyan invited me up to sit on her porch.

"Is the hawthorn blooming?" she asked. "I can't see very well." It was, a vibrant carmine in hue. A tiny woman of 87, she told me about seasons long past. "This town was 3,000 people at one time, they tell me." Now about 100 live here. Her father used to own the Alpine Hotel, a success then and now. The courthouse attracted people to town—and sometimes the saloons delayed their departure.

In good time, on a sunny day, our party floated into the East Fork. Ray Ford and some of his friends had come. Two old friends from Berkeley, Julia Nicholson and David Paine, had joined us. The river, high and silty-green from snowmelt, carried us in a never-ending waltz, from one side to the other. Clear spring water streamed out of lush meadows. Snowcapped peaks, always visible in the open canyon, played hide-and-seek with us. In front of us at first, they seemed to leap behind us with the twisting of the river.

Julia bobbed along like a duck in a little yellow inflatable boat. Jeff Schloss and David, in kayaks, "surfed" back upstream in the foaming waves they had just run. Wearing his now-seasoned straw hat, Ray deftly guided the raft I was in. The lower East Carson is a sociable river. Close to the fast-growing area of Reno, and with no rapids rated above II, it draws crowds on weekends. We saw children under six and senior citizens in their seventies floating along. Our camp soon turned into a brightly colored tent city.

David, Julia, and I hiked downstream, with gray jays scolding us, and dabbled our feet in a hot spring. "I've been on this river a dozen times," David said; "I really like the Carson." He described a trip far into the headwaters, to Carson Falls: "It's beautiful. An incredible narrows. And farther upstream the river is like a silver ribbon, coming off Sonora Peak."

Although I never got that far, I went trail riding near the upper reaches of the East Carson with a guide named Mark Bergstrom. I had not been on a horse in years; it seemed a long way down from atop Fallon, a sturdy 17-hand roan. I clamped my knees tight. We rode through meadows filled with lupine and iris, skirting treacherous bogs that could mean death to an unwary animal. Aspens clustered by rushing streams; some stood stark and gray, beaver-killed.

We forded Silver King Creek, in full spate, with Fallon lurching and sliding on the rocks and icy water surging over my feet, and picnicked in a meadow beside the East Fork, a narrow rushing stream. The scent of the horses mingled with the resin of the pines. Strange, waxy red flowers called snow plants, found only in alpine areas, pushed up through the humus.

On another day Shane Murphy, founder of the Carson River Conservation Fund, invited me for a raft trip. His shaggy beard seems more appropriate to this land of miners and mountain men than to his native Philadelphia. Professional boatman, conservationist, and historian, Shane is the kind who would spend two weeks in the library just to find out who was hanged at Hangman's Bridge below Markleeville. That was one Ernst Reusch, who, in 1872, murdered E. H. Errickson for alienating the affection of his bride of two weeks. *(Continued on page 162)*

*B*eaver-killed aspens turn ghostly against pines and firs along the upper East Carson. From headwaters on Sonora Peak in the Sierra Nevada, the river tumbles northward through gorges and alpine meadows where livestock can graze in summer. Flowing out of California, it joins the main Carson on the desert plain of western Nevada. A gnarled juniper, typical of the lower river, clings to a rocky slope.

*P*rickly poppies gleam white in the sun in the upper watershed of the East Fork of the Carson. Mule-ears gild an alpine meadow. A century ago silver and gold ore brought riches to Carson country. Today fishermen and boaters find wealth in its free-flowing river. "It's a very sociable river on weekends," the author found, "accessible from many urban areas. I saw boatmen, old and young and of a wide range of skills, all there for real outdoors fun."

Shane knows not only every detail of the Carson's past, but also its every rock and rapid. Armed with paddles, we set out. "Forward, stroke, one," a quiet command would come. "Back, two!" We dug our paddles into the water and slid down the chute between two boulders, or skirted a "strainer"—debris or trees lodged in the river. A strainer can hold a boat or person trapped as the water pours through. At normal flows this section of the upper East Fork earns a good III, but at high water Shane simply terms it "deadly."

"Forward!" Shane punctuated the tempo of the river with bits of history. We entered a sinuous section: "Lord Chalmers Rapid—Lord Chalmers, two strokes forward, was an Englishman who invested at Silver Mountain in the 1860s, back one. He wasn't really a lord, but he impressed the local people with his money and his big house."

Now a proposed high dam would turn most of the East Carson into a reservoir. Shane's group hopes to preserve the free-flowing river and to develop water-management policy for parched western Nevada. I studied their plans as I headed for different country: northern California, which has water in abundance.

I felt a little like Alice, turned suddenly tiny. I wandered through waist-high sword ferns and craned to see the tops of redwoods 250 feet above me. Even the rhododendrons were giants, 20 or 30 feet tall, in pink and mauve glory. I had heard the Smith River called the "crown jewel" of the whole Wild and Scenic System. I knew why in an instant, when I saw the water, an astonishing aquamarine color, flowing silently in Jedediah Smith Redwoods State Park. Two mergansers dived for fish through water so clear that every rock and pebble could be seen a good fathom down. Water striders padded across the surface on their big feet. Their shadows, even bigger, chased them along the bottom.

The Smith River system spills out of the Siskiyou Mountains and cuts across the northwest corner of California to the foggy Pacific shore. In 1828, Jedediah Smith, for whom the river is named, fought his way up the coast through nearly impenetrable redwood forest. Easter-lily farms cover logged-over areas on the lower Smith today, but as yet no dams check these waters.

Tributaries of the Smith—more than three-quarters of the watershed—web the northern part of the Six Rivers National Forest. One sunny day I followed a trail high above the South Fork with resources officer Richard Pickenpaugh and his German wirehaired pointer, Blitz. The turquoise water teased us with glimpses, between enormous old cedars and firs, as it spilled from pool to pool. The delicate, sweet-gingery scent of wild azaleas permeated the air. Sometimes, close to the river, we walked in iris-filled meadows. Pick reeled off the names of other flowers: fairy bells, monkey flowers, blue brodiaea.

I teetered on a log across a creek; Blitz trotted confidently behind. At Eightmile Creek there was no log and we could go no farther. We lunched in the sunshine while a merganser and her six tiny ducklings bobbed past in the swirling water.

On another sunny day I sat with Chris Souza on the deck of her house, watching the riffling Middle Fork at Gasquet. A bubbly blonde, she told me that "A young man from New York once asked me, 'What do you put in the water to make it that color?' I could not convince him we don't add anything."

"That's the way rivers are supposed to look," added her husband, Ted. Retired in name only, the Souzas fish commercially; they keep bees, a big garden, canaries, and a beagle named T. C. Ted is the Gasquet fire chief; Chris sits on the North Coast water quality board. Both work with environmental groups that watchdog the Smith River. We discussed the problems indiscriminate logging and road-building can cause. "People here think the river never changes," Ted remarked. "It's like looking in the mirror—we never look any older. Then you see a picture taken twenty years before, and you've changed."

Toward evening we scrambled down an embankment to fish in the Middle Fork. With a graceful flick of his wrist, Ted sent the hook and lure into a deep pool. "I've fished these North Coast waters for steelhead for 35 years," he said; "the Smith is the last stand." (Steelhead are oceangoing rainbow trout.) "We have a tremendous big strain of steelhead here—the state record of 27.5 pounds."

In what I thought was a fair imitation of Ted's style, I hooked an alder on the bank. Ted came over to untangle me. "Here, hold this rod—there's a fish on it." Sure enough, a steelhead flopped to the surface. Huge, of course. Ted gently unhooked it and slipped it back. "I keep only what I can eat." He went on: "I've tried to talk to the commercial salmoners about the importance of spawning habitat. Very few seem to understand. They think God just dumps 'em out there!" A few more attempts at casting, and I noticed that Ted and Chris had moved farther down the bank away from me.

For whatever reason, though still more numerous than in most rivers, the steelhead and salmon in the Smith have declined noticeably since the 1950s. Joe Moreau, a young fishery biologist for the Forest Service, places some blame on a major flood in 1964 that washed out some of the spawning beds and buried others, and some on commercial ocean fishing. "It's estimated that three to five king salmon are caught in the ocean for every one that makes it back here." And of the historic waters for anadromous fish, many are now blocked by dams. We had driven up the Middle Fork to Patrick Creek to see how the Forest Service is restoring some of the spawning beds. Joe pointed to gabions— wire cages filled with rock, V-shaped downstream, to catch and hold gravel. "This idea has been in use for hundreds of years. The Romans used wicker baskets to reinforce riverbanks. It has worked incredibly well here."

In a county like Del Norte, dependent on logging and fishing, with unemployment approaching 30 percent, it's hard to fight a company that might bring jobs. I talked with William Hosken, president of California Nickel, about plans for a cobalt mine on Gasquet Mountain. These call for a dam on Copper Hill Creek.   *(Continued on page 168)*

FOLLOWING PAGES: *"It's mine," a river otter seems to say with a paw on its half-eaten dinner on the bank of the Smith River in northern California. Fishermen take record salmon and steelhead in the near-pristine Smith and its tributaries.*

*F*lag *warns of divers below in the clear waters of the Smith. "Gold is much better than green money," says Earl Stanley, displaying nuggets from the river. Working only four months a year, "so as not to interfere with any salmon or steelhead runs," Earl and his partners vacuum through bottom gravel. Gold mining here dates from the 1850s. Today controversy flares about the harm surface mining for cobalt might do to the river's extraordinary water quality.*

"I know we won't do any harm," he told me. "I know nobody will let us do harm!" A vigorous man in his 60s, he repudiated any thought of damage from the dam. "That's a dry creek most of the time." It would, however, set a precedent: first dam in the entire Smith River system. Opponents fear the impact of flour-fine tailings on the pristine water, of a processing plant's coal emissions on the air.

In 1981, to preserve the watershed and the fishery, the whole Smith River and some of its tributaries were designated wild and scenic. Now timber interests—and the southern California water interests—may succeed in getting the designation ended. And California risks losing its last untrammeled river system.

"Standing like two spectres . . . emaciated," scarcely recognizable, the Astorians found John Day and a companion near the Columbia River. The two men had fallen ill and split off from the main group of John Jacob Astor's 1811-1812 exploration party to make their own way. Attacked by Indians, they had lost everything, including their clothing. John Day's name lives today on a river that cuts through Oregon's arid center.

At its headwaters in the Blue Mountains of eastern Oregon, the John Day starts small, easily spanned with one long step as it meanders through meadows and forests. It broadens to flow through ranches and farms, then cuts into basalt canyons. Finally, 284 miles later, it spills into the Columbia. The river with its tributaries drains more than 8,000 square miles. This area is sparsely populated, and becoming more so. Abandoned farmhouses dot the landscape. "Now the young men are being squeezed out—the people we really need," a wheat farmer told me. "Machine prices have gone up 15 times what they were around 1960; farm products have only doubled."

I joined Mary K. Campbell and her uncle for a trip along the North Fork, where he ranches. Apple orchards in neat rows gave the bottomland the texture of intricate crewel embroidery. Mary K., a rancher's daughter with dark hair and a gamine face, had once traveled in Ireland. "All that green was nice," she told me, "but I like the kind of beauty we have here, the dry beauty."

The air chilled as we climbed higher. The road leveled onto a high plateau, 4,500 feet up. We could see creeks that flow down to the Middle Fork of the John Day. Shadows of thunderclouds skimmed across meadows tinged in soft shades of blue and green and gold.

Tom Campbell has the fair coloring and chiseled features—and the reticence—of many of the Celts who settled near the river. But as we drove along he warmed into story after story. He identified each mountain and rock outcropping: Dixie Butte, Opal Butte, Indian Rock. "There was an old lady who lived over there." Tom pointed to a house on a ridge. "The hogs got under her house and distorted the floor. She had to saw the legs off her table at one end to level it. When the harvest crew came, the tall ones knelt at the short end and the short ones stood at the tall end."

As a logger sees board feet in a tree, a farmer sees crops and forage in water. "The North Fork is a multipurpose river, not wild and scenic," Tom remarked. But in its rocky gorges—national forest land—it seemed wild, running clear and full. Rain clouds turned the water to silver against the dark Douglas firs. Tom talked about growing up in this country, herding sheep in the summer. When had he switched from sheep to cattle? "When the coyotes ate the last one, I guess."

Sheep aren't the only animals to have had a tough time in John Day country. Twenty-five million years ago, huge cats preyed on sheep-like herbivores called oreodonts. Rhinoceroses, camels, and saber-toothed cats roamed the area, then a well-watered inland basin. Layers of volcanic ash gradually filled the basin and preserved a unique fossil record.

I followed Dr. John Ruben of Oregon State University up a steep creekside trail at Blue Basin in the John Day Fossil Beds National Monument. The pale blue-green canyon walls resembled crumbling sandcastles. "What you get in most fossil sites is a snapshot in time," said the young paleontologist. "You may cover a thousand years. Here you cover millions. This is a moving picture by comparison." Through the middle layers of the John Day formation, the deposits were continuous for six or eight million years. "That's very unusual," said John. "So what you are able to do here, at least with animals, is study the evolution of one particular lineage, whether rodents, or cats, or whatever." He showed me casts of fossil remains, an oreodont and a tortoise, placed where the bones were found. A saber-toothed cat the size of a lynx would be next.

It's a relief, I thought later as I spread my sleeping bag under the stars, that there are no more of those stabbing cats on the John Day. The moon had come up. Its light turned the riffling water to hammered silver. The scent of sagebrush filled the air.

*E*arlier I had made a raft trip with guide John Laing, down a 26-mile stretch of the lower John Day. John and Sherla Collins, who own the cattle ranch where we put in, came to see us off. A man with an ageless, sun-ruddy face, John Collins had served on the advisory committee that considered the John Day for national wild and scenic status. Part of the river is already an Oregon Scenic Waterway. Though Oregon's is considered one of the best state river systems, it cannot halt federal dam projects.

"I wanted to keep it in the state system," he said. "The farther away government gets from you, the harder it is. I wanted to protect my land." Echoing a point I would hear often, he added, "We farmers have to be good conservationists to stay in business."

Local farmers depend on the John Day's water. Often, by summer's end, there is not enough. But now there was plenty. The river was high, fast, green-brown with eroded silt. It curved through irrigated benches. Pumps poked through the willows on the banks. We could hear the hum of swathers in the hayfields. Whiteface calves scampered off into the juniper and sagebrush.

In the hillsides beyond we could see red layers and green ones of the John Day formation. At one spot, we broke off chunks of sedimentary rock that flaked like French pastry and revealed fossil leaves. Cliff swallows swooped from their gourdlike mud nests to protest our passing. A red-tailed hawk shrieked *(Continued on page 178)*

"*A*lmost narrow enough to cross in one big step," the upper John Day River seemed to the author, "as it looped through meadows and spilled over rocky drops." The Oregon river begins its 284-mile-journey in the forested Blue Mountains, then heads across dry terrain to the Columbia River. A bachelor's button peeks out from grass called Medusa head, a weed baneful to ranchers because its hairlike awns tax the digestive systems of cattle brought to summer grazing in the John Day's high country. Horsetail rushes grow in clumps around granite boulders in a tributary creek. The author found, along the John Day, ranching families with an openness and warm humor born of a closeness to their land and to the river.

Thunderclouds darken a midsummer sky over upland pasture near the John Day River. Wild flowers cover a broken-down fence in a meadow.

FOLLOWING PAGES: *"A vast volcanic layer cake," some call the ash-and-lava formations along the John Day known as the Painted Hills.*

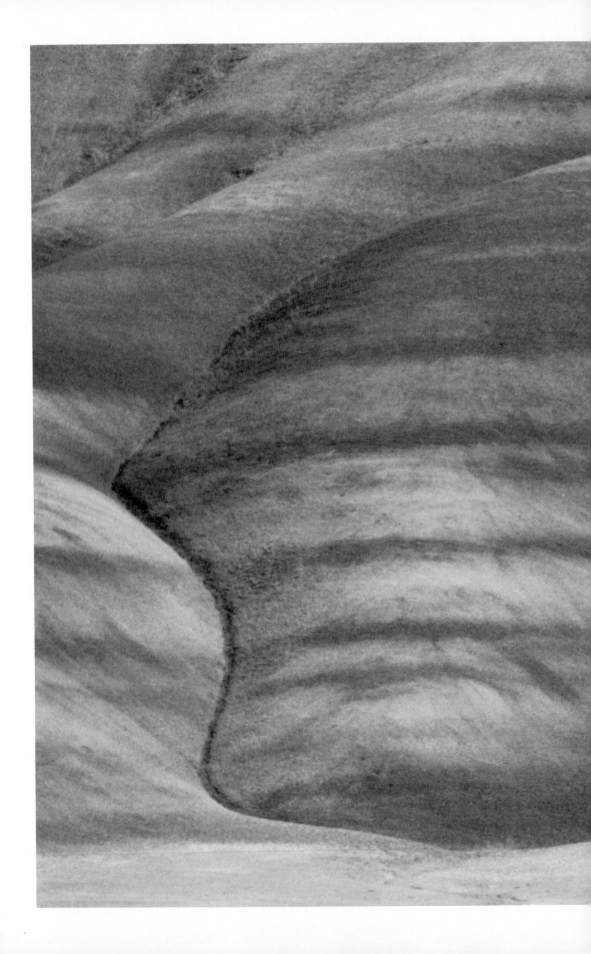

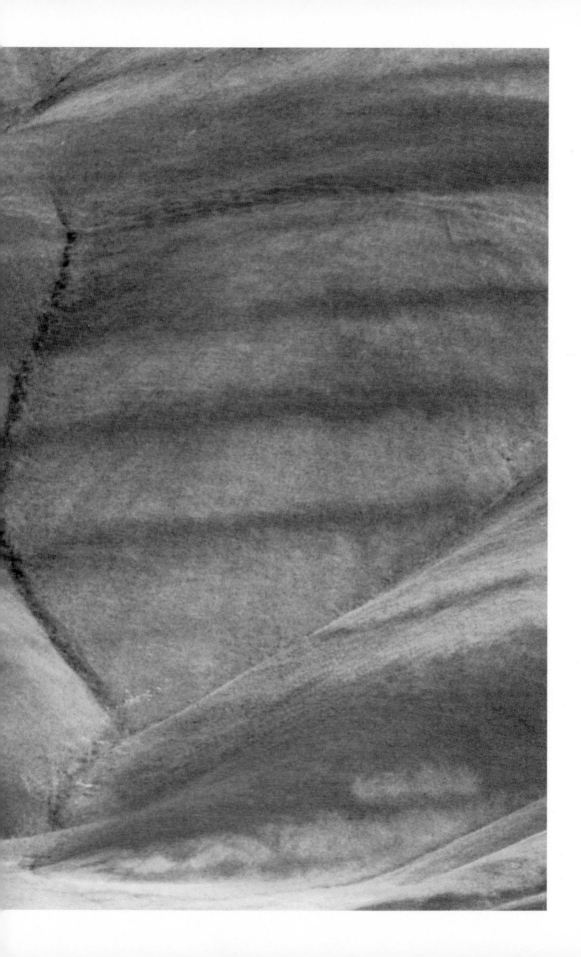

*"I*t's a good life, a good area to raise children," says John W. Re, a rancher on the lower John Day. He and his family ride near the ranch his wife's great-grandfather homesteaded in 1863. Water from the river irrigates alfalfa fields on the rich bottomland. In this area, ruts still remain from the Oregon Trail.

incantations from a basalt-capped outcropping called Cathedral Rock. The only other boats we saw were a couple of canoes; road access is scant in all the 157 miles of the lower John Day, and only about 2,000 people come boating in a year.

Later I ventured farther down the John Day with Paul Smith, a stocky part-time guide in his twenties, and a local wheat farmer, Bob Maley. The canyon below Clarno becomes deeper, the formations more spectacular. Terraced palisades became medieval citadels in our imagination. Pinnacles turned into Egyptian deities or Chinese empresses, basalt columns into soldiers guarding an ancient fortress.

A spare man nearing 60, with blue eyes that squint from years in the sun, Bob had never been on this part of the John Day. "It's a very fine river," he would say as he sprawled, totally relaxed, on one of the tubes of the raft.

Too soon, it was the last morning. We heard an unearthly scream as we shoved off—perhaps a lynx or a bobcat, Bob thought. Across the river on a rocky bar were two coyote pups howling at the blue skies.

If the John Day country has a dry beauty, the Hoh's is a drenched one. The rain began as I drove through an eerie forest of giant cedar, hemlock, and Sitka spruce. I caught a glimpse of the Olympic Mountains rising abruptly from the coastal plain, peaks swathed in heavy cloud. The Hoh River begins its 56-mile journey as melt from a glacier on Mount Olympus. It cuts through a black sandstone gorge before widening to run to the Pacific. Facing almost due west, its U-shaped valley catches the full impact of westerly winds, which shed their moisture to sustain a rare temperate rain forest.

On one of the few bright days I would see, I floated with a guide named Roger Hershner on the milky-gray waters of the Hoh, below Olympic National Park. The more the sun shines on the glaciers, he told me, the siltier the river becomes with glacial "flour"—rock scraped to powder by the ice. We had to watch for dangerous debris, even huge trees washed downstream. Sometimes the gravel-strewn river seeks new twists in its braids: "I've seen it move a quarter of a mile," remarked Roger, "from one side of the valley to the other."

The river is not the only thing on the Olympic Peninsula with independent ways. Residents complain that half of the land is in federal hands. We discussed the prospects for wild and scenic status for the Hoh. "People have this terrible feeling," Roger explained, "of being closed out. They think 'wild and scenic' is just more of that. They don't want legislators who know nothing about the situation to come in and impose their will."

We stopped at Maple Creek. I was beginning to learn the trees: hemlock, with graceful curving branches uniform to the top; Douglas fir, less evenly shaped; western red cedar, with lacy needles and shaggy bark. Roger handed me a branch. I grabbed it—ouch! Sharp needles jabbed my fingers. "That's how you tell Sitka spruce!"

Spruce needles and salmonberry branches slapped across my face as I rode the Hoh River Trail following Marilyn Brown, granddaughter of local pioneers, her daughter Emmi, and two of their friends. "Bears have been here—it's a smell like rancid fat," Marilyn remarked as we rode along a narrow ledge a hundred feet above the gray-swirling river. At times the trail wound away from the river under a 250-foot-high canopy of hemlock and spruce. Sword ferns and bracken brushed our legs. "Nurse" logs, fallen a century or more, supported colonnades of younger trees. Soft veils of club moss, draped from the trees, caught shafts of light and turned to gold. There were lichens that looked like lettuce, and ferns that tasted like licorice. And in this enchanted forest, an extraordinary silence reigned, as if all sound—except the occasional trilling of a thrush and the clicking of our horses' hooves—were absorbed into the cushioning plants.

The Hoh Indians feared this upper river. In their belief, this was the home of the dreaded Thunderbird. Whenever people came too near, he sent chunks of ice thundering off the glaciers. Yet their identification with the river goes far beyond sharing a name. The river and the fish in it form the core of their culture. The Salmon Bringer, a boy captured by the salmon, is central in their mythology. He returns to tell the Hoh they may catch salmon, but should return the bones to the river to assure more fish in future.

Today the Hoh Tribe holds a tiny, 443-acre reservation at the mouth of the river. Like other tribes the Hoh, in the 1850s, relinquished by treaty most of their lands. In return they were assured the right to fish and hunt in "all the usual and accustomed grounds." Since then they have often been prevented from exercising that right. And they have been blamed for a decline in the fishery—despite non-Indian factors: intensive commercial fishing; runoff from logging on the Hoh, industrial pollution and dam building on other rivers.

In the 1970s, federal courts upheld the treaty rights and awarded the Indians the right to 50 percent of the harvestable fish. Ever since, as one sports fisherman put it, "A lot of people are ready to go to war with the Indian again." Now the fight is over steelhead.

At Forks, a town filled with burly loggers, I met Craig Hunley, of the Olympic Peninsula Guides Association. "The Hoh River is in a class by itself," Craig told me. "It's a very, very good river." He listed the attractions: summer steelhead, spring salmon, fall salmon, and more. Craig admits that the Indians are not the sole cause of the decline of the steelhead. They do make a visible target for blame, netting fish at the mouth of the river, though sportsmen take many steelhead and the non-Indian saltwater fleet takes many more salmon. He thinks one solution would be to "buy out the Indian fishing rights completely," though he says, "I don't believe we owe them anything."

The Indians ask: "How can a people be compensated for the destruction of their culture and their future?"

To see what the Hoh are doing to preserve both, I pulled on hip-waders and slogged through alders into a cold creek. Jim Jorgensen, a non-Indian, is the tribe's fishery biologist. He showed me a plywood-and-wire-mesh maze, set up to help him tag the young fish before they head to sea; the tags let him monitor the population. Generally a low-key sort, Jim becomes fervent on this subject: "The Indian intent is to maintain their traditional fishery. It's to their advantage to have proper management." He pointed out that the sports fishermen can travel far and wide to fish. The Hoh must stay here. But I had to leave.

*I*t was nice to see the sun and dry out a little. I headed east from Lewiston, Idaho, up the Clearwater from its confluence with the Snake. The Middle Fork of the Clearwater, and the Selway and Lochsa Rivers, made up a so-called "instant river" in the National Wild and Scenic System, included at once upon passage of the 1968 Act.

Almost like twin streams, the Selway and the Lochsa rise in the Bitterroot Mountains that straddle the Idaho-Montana border. They tumble through rocky gorges, then converge to form the Clearwater's Middle Fork. A road parallels the Lochsa for almost its entire length, providing easy access for fishermen, boaters, and campers. The Selway lies pristine, remote in the heart of the Selway-Bitterroot Wilderness, with only a trail alongside it.

Tidy farms and homesteads line the narrow flatlands along the Middle Fork. Local people swim and boat here in summer. In the early '60s most residents favored the wild and scenic designation, because it would save their homes from inundation by a dam.

Before there were white men to squabble over the land along the Clearwater, the Nez Perce were here—as early as 12,000 years ago. I followed Angus Wilson along the river. A big-boned, handsome man, a historian and something of an elder statesman for the tribe, Angus pointed out rocks in the river that are linked with myths. "Coyote is a wise and foolish animal," he said. "Every legend has Coyote in it, whether the good side or bad side of him." Rocky outcroppings upstream represent parts of a monster that Coyote killed. The Nez Perce, legend holds, sprang from the Monster's heart blood.

Angus pointed to a hill far across the river where Chief Joseph had come in 1877, in flight from Gen. O. O. Howard, and told me that his grandfather had given food to the refugees. For a while I followed the route of Chief Joseph's band as I drove over Lolo Pass to the "other side"—Montana—bound for my first trip on the Selway. The road is narrow and lonely, except for trucks barreling around curves fifty feet above the Lochsa River; I had a sense of the unknown.

That mood pervades the Selway, one of the most unspoiled and exciting white-water rivers in the country. To be on it is, literally, a privilege. During the short season, to preserve fragile campsites and the quality of experience, the Forest Service allows only one group a day—with a maximum of 16 people—to put in. Commercial outfitters are allotted a total of 16 trips for their customers. Private boaters must try a lottery. Some people wait years to get on. We were fortunate.

Gary Lockrow, of Flagstaff, Arizona, had a permit and space to share. My friends David and Julia came from Berkeley with their raft, Ray Ford from Santa Barbara with his. Several of Gary's group were professional oarsmen, with two oarswomen. We had six rafts and three kayaks in all. None of us had much knowledge of the Selway, but soft-spoken Gary would be a good leader.

A pika bade us a high-pitched farewell *(Continued on page 186)*

Cascade spills over moss-covered rocks to meet the Hoh River on the Olympic Peninsula. The Hoh flows to dense rain forest from an Ice Age world of glaciers and perpetual snow on Mount Olympus—the wettest part of the contiguous U. S.

"*The river has a mind of its own,*" *says a native of Hoh country. At high flows the stream cuts new channels through the forest, toppling Sitka spruces and western hemlocks—some nearly 200 feet high—and leaving benches of gravel. This stretch of the river provides prime salmon and steelhead spawning beds.*

*"I*f we don't teach the children, they will lose the tradition," says Pansy Hudson, an elder of the Hoh Tribe. In a day-long demonstration of old ways to prepare food, she bakes bread in fire-heated sand. Seated on driftwood, families await a seafood dinner on the shore at the mouth of the Hoh. The link between the Hoh and their river goes deep, as the author discovered.

when we put in at White Cap Creek. We floated through deep, forested canyon. Light filtered through lacy needles of huge shaggy cedars. The water, clear and green, was swift. *Sal-wah* means "sound of water flowing" in Nez Perce, Angus Wilson had told me. It seemed appropriate as the river riffled along. Our kayakers frolicked in the waves like otters. "It's the most sensual sport," one told me. "I feel totally one with the water."

At one camp I crossed the river to meet Sarah Barlow and her husband, Ian, the young caretakers at Running Creek Ranch. This is one of three homesteads still maintained on the Selway, all accessible only by trail or tiny airstrips. I watched Sarah roll out pastry for pies to be baked in an old woodburning range. Later, in a shed out back, she stirred something in an evil-looking brine. Ian had shot a black bear, and she was trying to cure the pelt. I asked her if the winters weren't long and lonely. "We read incredible amounts. But simply figuring things out is enough stimulation. The only thing is," she added with a laugh, "when you stay here all winter thinking, you begin to think all your opinions are right!"

One day I shared Sue Bassett's raft. Tall, without an extra ounce, Sue-B rows with a careful skill and grace acquired during ten years on the Colorado in the Grand Canyon. We slid down a glassy-smooth slot, a classic V-shape, at a rapid called Ham that rates a IV. It did not seem as difficult as some intricate passages upstream.

I asked Sue-B which river she likes best. "That's tough," she answered. "Each has its own character, something special. The Snake is so great—the power of Hells Canyon. I feel the presence of the Nez Perce. As if they never left the place."

They had been at Moose Creek, too, to harvest salmon, and called it Khaah-khaah-youk-ne-mah—Place of the Mountain Alders. We had barely set up our tents there when the rain began, no mere cloudburst. Rising mist off the river and dipping clouds transformed the slopes and peaks into a mysterious Tolkien world.

"Oh, for sure, Ladle is going to make me nervous," Ray Ford remarked. We were walking along the trail to scout the rapids. "It's the Lava of the little rivers." (Lava Falls is the biggest, scariest rapid in the Grand Canyon.) Zebra swallowtail butterflies swirled around us; we nibbled on thimbleberries. Then we were staring down at seething, boiling water. For a distance of 600 yards it was all white. Rocks everywhere, big rocks. And no smooth, V-shaped tongue to point the way. But Ray has a practiced eye: "There's an eddy there—that'll give you time to slow up and turn backwards to get a strong stroke to get you through the slot at center."

For nearly six miles below Moose Creek, resistant granite forces the Selway into great sweeping curves, its water a plunging maelstrom. There is hardly a place to pull over for scouting. It is this stretch that draws some of the best boatmen in the West. If some rapids are like a brief concerto, played fortissimo, this series on the Selway is like a whole symphony. And the boatman must know the entire score before he begins. Methodically, Ray made little drawings and notes of obstacles and the preferred route. He jotted down landmarks. He studied currents and cross-currents, the internal rhythm of the river.

While he worked, I hiked to Moose Creek Ranger Station. Entirely a wilderness district, Moose Creek is unique in the Forest Service. Penny and Emil Keck were sitting on the porch of their cabin. A bear of a man, somewhere around 70, with piercing blue eyes, Emil has lived here for 19 years. In the late 1950s he was a logger. When he refused to sign a petition against the Selway-Bitterroot Wilderness, the company let him go. He ended up at Moose Creek, in charge of fire control and trails and other facilities. He's retired now, and Penny, who is in her early 40s, holds his position. But now, as before, the Forest Service gets two for one. All along the river we had seen trails carefully maintained by Emil and Penny and the crews they supervise. "I can't leave here," he said, "because who will take care of this land? If you make one g.d. mistake, it's gone."

Penny finds it incomprehensible that "They want to put a dollar figure on wilderness—$1.91 an acre is what they came up with. There's no concept of any intangible value." By "they" she meant federal officials. I was never able to confirm a specific figure; but wilderness is consistently rated below land that can be exploited, and the issue haunts every discussion of wild places.

Wilderness means different things to different people. For some, simply, it is a pristine place, untrammeled by man. It is the solitude that draws others, loners who want a place to get away. But some find another dimension, an aspect well defined by conservationist Aldo Leopold. Wilderness gives the "complete freedom to make mistakes . . . the taste of those rewards and penalties for wise and foolish acts . . . against which civilization has built a thousand buffers." The Selway qualifies for all three definitions.

Our whole flotilla had nice, drenching rides in the first couple of rapids. I was in Ray's boat with Jean Collins, a young woman from California. At a rapid called Wa-Poots, The Rattlesnake, Ray made a spectacular run that took us up onto a water-covered boulder, then down and around with an expert pivot stroke. We were pretty high, elated and confident, as we pulled ashore to take a look at Ladle.

It would be the far right route. Jim Hendrick and his wife, Debra, went first for a beautiful run. Jim slipped past a large boulder upstream and paused—sure enough, there was an eddy in the middle. He turned his back to the center and pulled down between two large boulders. Sue-B and Gary made a graceful, dancing run. A Forest Service boat followed, without incident. Then one of our other boatmen chose the center. It looked like a wild, roller-coaster ride. I could see Ray's eyes light up. He was going to try it.

This time the butterflies were on the inside, and very active, as we shoved off. After a smooth entry at the center, we were suddenly snatched sideways to the left. We lurched sickeningly up against a huge rock. "High side!" Ray yelled. Jean and I leaped to the high side of the raft to bring it down. For a moment we paused.

Ray fought to get the raft around into position. We kept slipping farther left into a space among three immense boulders. We lingered on upwelling water. Then, in a split second, the water surged and slammed the boat against the largest rock. As we rose up tilting, I could see down that swirling left chute. Then over came the raft,

$\mathcal{K}$oos khee-ich-khee-ich, *"very clear water"* to the Nez Perce, the Middle Fork of the Clearwater basks in hot summer sun. According to their mythology, the Nez Perce sprang from the heart blood of a monster slain by Coyote along the river in central Idaho. The Clearwater gave explorers Lewis and Clark a westward route for canoes burned out Indian fashion, because their axes were "badly calculated to build·Canoes of the large Pine." Water splashes over rocks near shore. Maidenhair fern pushes up its delicate fronds along the banks. A spotted frog peers warily from a maze of aquatic plants.

crashing on top of us. I inhaled as much air as I could. The water ripped my sunglasses off. I was thrown violently, like a rag doll, in the darkness. Wave after wave of green-brown water welled up under the raft displacing the air as we smashed crazily from one rock to another. I couldn't breathe. I couldn't get out. If I came up at the wrong spot I could be crushed between raft and rock. Or the raft could "wrap" on a rock—stop with me pinned under it. Trapped.

Suddenly there was calm. Air. I pushed myself out into the sunshine. Ahead was a foaming drop. It was a relief to act. I remembered years of instruction: keep your feet up and pointed downstream, float on your back, paddle with your arms. . . .

"Grab hold." John Skeoch, one of our kayakers, had paddled over. Jean was already on the beach. The Forest Service crew had caught our boat and picked her up, too stunned to help herself. Ray had reached a rock, and was able to swim to safety.

We were lucky. The raft was unscathed, almost all the gear still tied on. The river selected appropriate tribute: Ray's cherished straw hat, and the wine we'd brought to celebrate getting through. That night in camp, the Forest Service group joined us around our fire; we thanked their boatman, Barry Miller, for their crew's fast action. Ray mulled over what had happened. "It's taking the time to study the run. . . . I just didn't do what I should have done. Rapids, they are all capable of munching you."

*L*ater I had the chance to fly back in to the Selway with my friends Dick and Sarah Walker. A lean, bearded forester, Dick has spent many years exploring the Selway country. We left the logged-over stretches, clear-cut slopes that looked moth-eaten. Then the wilderness seemed to stretch forever. Barren crags jutted up from forested canyons. We could see streams twisting through the rugged land.

And then we saw the Selway, silver in the early morning light, dwarfed by the expanse of forest and mountain. For a couple of days we hiked along the river and up Bear Creek. We swam in the creek's cold, blue-green depths, sharing a pool with several big steelhead. Flowers bloomed everywhere in the park-like forest: magenta clarkia, scarlet gilia, purple fireweed.

On the last evening, at twilight, we sat on the porch of Selway Lodge watching the river with Freddie and Everett Peirce. They used to run a guest ranch near Aspen. Then it got too crowded there. After searching for seven years, they came here. "When we first flew in, it had a very special feeling," Freddie told me. "I knew this was it. The river here is what is so magnificent. There is a feeling of peace that just seems to wash over you. All of a sudden you feel at peace." I looked at the river rippling past in the last glimmer of light, and I too felt that peace flow around me.

River's birth, snowmelt streams over mosses and ferns to feed a tributary of the Selway. The Selway remains one of America's most untouched wild rivers, for the most part accessible only by trails, in the heart of Idaho's vast wilderness.

*G*rand finale for a river comes at Selway Falls, 20 miles above the confluence with the Clearwater. The Selway thunders through a narrows impassable for boaters. Upstream, the six-mile stretch below Moose Creek ranks in the top white water of the United States, a challenge for expert kayakers like John Skeoch (below). By a maneuver called a "brace," he avoids capsizing in the welling froth below Ladle, the major runnable rapid on the Selway. The author's friend Dick Walker writes that Ladle gives the kayaker "an opportunity to share a kinship with the water ouzel, bobbing up and down as he hops and dives." It proved easier for kayaks than for rafts: The author's boat flipped over here.

FOLLOWING PAGES: *Dwarfed by a river on the rampage, kayakers pick their way among Ladle's granite boulders. To boaters and hikers, fishermen and hunters, the Selway offers a solitude rare even for America's wild rivers.*

Notes on Contributors

Free-lance photojournalist MATT BRADLEY, a resident of Little Rock and now a publisher, graduated from the U. S. Air Force Academy and discovered photography as a pilot. He has illustrated three books on Arkansas. His assignments for the Society have often involved canoeing; in March 1977 the magazine published his coverage of the Buffalo National River, first stream in the U. S. so strongly protected by law.

Hawaii-born free lance RICHARD A. COOKE III, who holds a graduate degree in architecture, has had varied "outdoor" photographic assignments for the Society. Among them is a chapter for *Canada's Wilderness Lands*. He found river trips a new experience—and hopes to do more. In 1983 he married Bronwyn James; they live in Eugene, Oregon.

BILL CURTSINGER, a free-lance specialist in underwater photography, has had numerous natural history assignments for the Society since 1972. He illustrated *Wake of the Whale*, written by Kenneth Brower, and John McPhee's *The Pine Barrens*. His career highlights include a one-man show in Paris in 1982. He and his family live in Portland, Maine.

Born in Puerto Rico, now resident in Virginia, LOUIS DE LA HABA graduated from Amherst College, received an M.A. in anthropology from the George Washington University. As a staff member and then as a free-lance writer, he has had numerous Society assignments on wilderness or archaeological topics, ranging from the Canadian Shield to ancient Mesoamerica and Southeast Asia.

Fond of canoeing since childhood, TONI EUGENE grew up in Pennsylvania, majored in English at and graduated from Gettysburg College, and joined the Society's staff in 1971. She has been a secretary, researcher, and caption writer for Special Publications, and wrote its children's book *Strange Animals of Australia*.

Born in Missouri, RALPH GRAY graduated from the University of Maryland; he joined the Society's staff in 1943, and has written numerous articles for NATIONAL GEOGRAPHIC. Editor of the children's magazine *World* since 1975, he formerly edited its predecessor *School Bulletin*. His assignments have included rivers featured in this book as well as the Susquehanna and its tributary Pine Creek, the Sangamon, the Grand Canyon, the Hamilton (now the Churchill) and the Unknown in Labrador. He lives in Maryland.

LAWRENCE F. MOSHER, a graduate of Stanford University, reported on the Middle East from Beirut from 1964 through 1967, then on things American for *National Observer*. He spent two years as writer in residence at the Georgetown University Center for Contemporary Arab Studies. He now covers environmental affairs for *National Journal*; in 1982 the National Wildlife Federation named him Communicator of the Year. He lives in Washington, D. C.

White-water buff JENNIFER C. URQUHART, a native of the Washington area, graduated from Smith College and attended the University of London. She spent two years in Australia, as a research assistant at the University of Sydney. A Special Publications staff member since 1973, she has been a researcher and caption writer, and is author of the children's book *Animals That Travel*.

Widely traveled free-lance photographer STEVE WALL, of Rutherfordton, N.C., majored in psychology at Temple College while working full time for Chattanooga newspapers. He has covered scenes of conflict in the Middle East and Northern Ireland. This is his first assignment for Special Publications—and his "first time in wild, wild country like the Selway's."

STEVE WALL

Freshly scrubbed after rugged wear, socks dry in the sun on a Selway River homestead—symbols of hard work to many who live along America's wild rivers, tokens of comfort to all who cheerfully get splashed or doused pursuing happiness along her scenic streams.

Acknowledgments

The Special Publications Division is grateful to the individuals, groups, and organizations named and quoted in the text and to those cited here for their generous assistance during the preparation of this book. State officials and agencies have helped in innumerable ways, as have personnel of the Smithsonian Institution, the U. S. Army Corps of Engineers, the U. S. Forest Service, the Bureau of Land Management, the Bureau of Mines, the Bureau of Reclamation, and, in particular, the National Park Service.

Chapter 1: Sioux Baldwin, Deborah A. Bell, R. Clifford Black IV, James W. Carrico, Jon and Tom Dragan, J. Glenn Eugster, John Fischer, Dr. Ives Goddard, Dr. John T. Hack, Allen Haden, Hilarie Jones, Arthur Miller, Jonathan Miller, Erskine and Jackie Pugh, H. Stephen Snyder, Chris Wallen, Walter R. T. Witschey, Wayne Yonkelwitz; Wildwater Expeditions Unltd.

Chapter 2: John Besse, E. Suzanne Carter, Dr. A. Tyrone Harrison, Charles J. Killebrew, Francis G. Koenig, David H. Riskind; the River Recreation Association of Texas.

Chapter 3: Lou George, Gregg B. Harmon, Dana Hill, Polly Schaafsma, George A. Woolsey, Jr.

Chapter 4: Jon B. Bledsoe, Morton Brigham, Richard and Robin Hildner, James R. Huddlestun, Benjamin F. Ladd, Doris Milner, Philip N. Osborn, Doug Peterson, Herb Spradlin, Kenneth Wolfinbarger, Howard Yanish.

Throughout: John Haubert, Dr. William V. Sliter; American Rivers Conservation Council.

INDEX

Boldface indicates illustrations
Italic refers to picture captions

Additional Reading

The reader may want to consult the *National Geographic Index;* since 1888 the GEO-GRAPHIC has published many notable articles on rivers. Of related interest are the Society's book *Wilderness U.S.A.* and the Special Publications *Still Waters, White Waters, America's Majestic Canyons,* and *As We Live and Breathe: the Challenge of Our Environment.*

The National Park Service has prepared *The Nationwide Rivers Inventory,* key reference on rivers proposed for or included in the Wild and Scenic System.

The following may also be useful: William H. Amos, *Wildlife of the Rivers;* Norman Bancroft-Hunt and Werner Forman, *People of the Totem: The Indians of the Pacific Northwest;* John Francis Bannon, *The Spanish Borderlands Frontier 1513-1821;* Bruce Brown, *Mountain in the Clouds: A Search for the Wild Salmon;* Mark H. Brown, *The Flight of the Nez Perce;* Robert O. Collins and Roderick Nash, *The Big Drops: Ten Legendary Rapids;* Phyllis Flanders Dorset, *The New Eldorado: The Story of Colorado's Gold and Silver Rushes;* William O. Douglas, *A Wilderness Bill of Rights;* Philip Fradkin, *A River No More: The Colorado River and The West;* Frank Gruber, *Zane Grey;* Samuel G. Houghton, *A Trace of Desert Waters: The Great Basin Story;* Verne Huser, *River Camping: Touring by Canoe, Raft, Kayak, and Dory;* Michael Jenkinson, *Wilderness Rivers of America;* Elizabeth A. H. John, *Storms Brewed in Other Men's Worlds: The Confrontation of Indians, Spanish, and French in the Southwest, 1540-1795;* John M. Kauffmann, *Flow East: A Look at Our North Atlantic Rivers;* Janet Lecompte, *Pueblo, Hardscrabble, Greenhorn: The Upper Arkansas, 1832-1856;* Henry Lumpkin, *From Savannah to Yorktown;* Roderick Nash, *Wilderness and the American Mind;* Jonathan Raban, *Old Glory: An American Voyage;* William Faulkner Rushton, *The Cajuns;* Mari Sandoz, *Old Jules;* Polly Schaafsma, *Indian Rock Art of the Southwest;* Ann Schafer, *Canoeing Western Waterways: The Coastal States;* John Seelye, *Prophetic Waters: The River in Early American Life and Literature;* Thomas F. Waters, *The Streams and Rivers of Minnesota.*

Library of Congress ⬚ Data
Main entry under title:

America's wild and scenic rivers.

Bibliography: p.
Includes index.
1. Wild and scenic rivers—
United States. 2. United States—
Description and travel—1981-
I. National Geographic Society
(U. S.).   Special Publications Division.
QH76.A46 1983   508.73   83-47843

ISBN 0-87044-440-9 (regular binding)

ISBN 0-87044-445-X (library binding)

Composition for *America's Wild and Scenic Rivers* by National Geographic's Pho-
tographic Services, Carl M. Shrader, Director, Lawrence F. Ludwig, Assistant
Director. Printed and bound by Holladay-Tyler Printing Corp., Rockville, Md.
Color separations by the Lanman Progressive Co., Washington, D. C.; Lincoln
Graphics, Inc., Cherry Hill, N.J.; NEC, Inc., Nashville, Tenn.; Sterling Regal,
Inc., New York, N.Y.

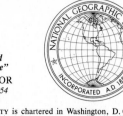